COLE'S KITCHEN ARTS SERIES

Classic Techniques
FOR • FINE • COOKING

FAYE LEVY
Writer

MICHAEL LAMOTTE
Photographer

COLE
GROUP

Faye Levy, a native of Washington, D.C., spent five years at La Varenne, the famous Parisian cooking school, where she earned the Grand Diplôme and worked as the cookbook editor. She has also worked and studied in Israel. A nationally syndicated columnist for the *Los Angeles Times* since 1990, she has been the culinary-technique columnist for *Bon Appétit* magazine. She has authored cookbooks in French, Hebrew, and English, and is a cooking teacher and a frequent contributor to *Gourmet* and other national food magazines and to major newspapers throughout the country. She and her husband and associate, Yakir Levy, currently are residents of Santa Monica, California.

Front Cover Marinated Roast Veal With Spinach and Pine Nut Stuffing combines several techniques to produce an impressive main course. A veal roast is butterflied and marinated in rosemary, white wine, and olive oil before being stuffed, rolled, and roasted (page 106).

Title Page Versatile Fresh Tomato Sauce gets its rich flavor from fresh, ripe tomatoes (page 41). For ease in preparation, assemble all ingredients before beginning to cook the sauce.

Back Cover

Upper Outfit your kitchen with a basic collection of well-chosen, high-quality equipment (page 9).

Lower Creamy Baked Chocolate Custard (page 122) is easy to prepare using the techniques explained in the chapter on desserts (page 115).

Special Thanks to Bob's Supply Co., San Francisco, California; Commercial Aluminum Cookware Co., Toledo, Ohio; Cuisinarts, Inc., Greenwich, Connecticut; Dacor, Pasadena, California; Forrest Jones, San Francisco, California; Steve Roth, San Francisco, California; Williams-Sonoma, San Francisco, California

Cole books are available for quantity purchases for sales promotions, premiums, fund-raising, or educational use. For more information on Cole's Kitchen Arts Series or other Cole culinary titles, please write or call the publisher.

Contributors

Editors
Susan Lammers, Sally W. Smith

Additional Photographers
Laurie Black; Patricia Brabant, page 118; Yakir Levy, author; Bob Montesclaros, title page and back cover, top photograph

Photographic and Food Stylist
Amy Nathan

Additional Food Stylists
Jeff Van Hanswyk;
Olivia Erschen, page 118

Illustrator
Edith Allgood

Calligrapher
Chuck Wertman

Designers
Linda Hinrichs, Carol Kramer

The Cole's Kitchen Arts Series is published by the staff of Cole Group, Inc.

Publisher
Brete C. Harrison

VP and Director of Operations
Linda Hauck

VP Publishing
Robert G. Manley

VP Marketing and Business Development
John A. Morris

VP and Associate Publisher
James Connolly

Senior Editor
Annette Gooch

Editorial Assistant
Lynn Bell

Production Coordinator
Dotti Hydue

© 1995 Cole Group, Inc.

All rights reserved under international and Pan-American copyright conventions.

Printed in Hong Kong through Mandarin Offset.

G F E D C B A
1 0 9 8 7 6 5

ISBN 1-56426-071-2

Library of Congress Catalog Card Number 94-28039

Address all inquiries to
Cole Group, Inc.
1330 N. Dutton Ave., Suite 103
Santa Rosa, CA 95401
(800) 959-2717   (707) 526-2682
FAX (707) 526-2687

Distributed to the book trade by Publishers Group West.

C O N T E N T S

Beating egg whites properly, the key to light soufflés and mousses, is one of the few techniques that you need to master for good cooking.

Keys to Successful Cooking

Most cooking is based on a relatively small number of techniques. Once you understand these basics, recipes make sense because they fall into recognizable patterns. Each chapter in this book covers a set of related techniques, introduced by explanatory text and illustrated by recipes that utilize the procedures. By reading the text and preparing the dishes, you can master the classic techniques of cooking—and enjoy great food in the process!

STEP-BY-STEP TO SUCCESSFUL COOKING

Cooking is a creative, satisfying experience. It can also be complex: reading a recipe and trying to visualize the results, choosing the ingredients at the market, carrying out a number of steps to prepare the dish, making several dishes at once, adding the finishing touches of seasoning and garnish. When each step of the process is thoroughly understood and carried out with skill, the result is a feast for both eye and tongue: wonderful food that looks as good as it tastes. But it can take a professional chef years to acquire the techniques that produce such culinary masterpieces. Does that mean the home cook is doomed to disappointment? Of course not!

You will want to learn the fundamentals, but there is no need to master them all at once. Begin by cooking with simple recipes that you understand well. If you follow them attentively, the food will always be good. As you gain experience, you can become more adventuresome and attempt recipes that appear more complex.

In this book you will find careful explanations of cooking basics: stocks and soups; sauces; steaming, poaching, and boiling; sautéing and deep-frying; braising and stewing; roasting and grilling; and dessert techniques. The recipes, chosen to help you learn by doing, lead you through the techniques step by step. In addition, you will find illustrations of selected procedures.

This first chapter covers the preliminaries: planning a menu, considering seasoning, equipping the kitchen, a few garnishing techniques for enhancing presentation, and basic food-preparation techniques.

MENU PLANNING

Today's menus are flexible; they no longer follow a set sequence as in previous, more formal times. A meal can consist simply of a grilled meat accompanied by a salad and followed by fresh fruit for dessert, or it can be more elaborate and begin with a soup or appetizer, followed by a main course and several accompaniments, then a green salad, fine cheeses, and dessert.

Menu planning is an art and thus a reflection of personal taste. Many cooks choose the main course first and select the remaining courses to complement it. One hallmark of well-planned menus is good use of seasonal fruits and vegetables.

The key to a good menu is variety. There should be several different flavors, colors, textures, and shapes. It is best to picture how the main course and its accompaniments will look on the plate and to include at least one colorful food. A major ingredient or flavoring should not be repeated several times in the same meal. If, for example, the main course is rich and contains a creamy sauce, the appetizer and side dishes should not be rich and creamy also. The sequence is also important. A spicy appetizer, for instance, will overpower a delicate main course.

Timing should be considered so that dishes are ready when needed. At first, keep your menus simple and the timing uncomplicated. Planning is easiest if the menu includes at least one dish that can be prepared completely ahead and either served cold or reheated; avoid including several dishes that require last-minute attention. Many cooks prefer not to attempt more than one new dish in any single meal.

At formal dinners, every course may be accompanied by a different wine, but the most practical solution at home is to choose one wine that complements the main course. The basic rule is that seafood is served with dry white wine, dark meats such as beef and lamb are served with dry red wine, and poultry and light meats are served with either.

In the following two sample menus, the first courses and desserts can be made ahead for the most part. In the second menu, the main course can be prepared in advance as well. Omit the toasted almonds from the rice dish in the second menu—the first course already contains nuts.

SAMPLE MENUS

Menu I

*Country Watercress Soup
(page 24)*

*Roast Chicken With
Rice, Fruit, and
Almond Stuffing
(page 102)*

*Quick Buttered Cabbage
(page 67)*

*Basic Chocolate Mousse
(page 123)*

Menu II

*Beet Salad With Pecans
and Mixed Greens
(page 56)*

*Lamb Curry With Ginger
and Coconut Milk
(page 94)*

*Rice With Peas, Swiss Chard,
and Toasted Almonds
(page 65)*

Cooked Carrots

*Fruit Salad With Liqueur and
Whipped Cream
(page 117)*

THE ART OF SEASONING

Good cooking depends on careful seasoning. The amounts of salt and pepper added depend on the cook's taste and on the ingredients in the dish. It is essential to taste a dish whenever possible before serving. Of course, you cannot taste a large cut of meat for seasoning, but you can taste soups, sauces, or other liquids or mixtures of ingredients, except those containing raw pork. Generally, foods that will be served cold need more seasoning than those served hot because the seasoning in chilled foods is less evident. When tasting, consider what additional seasoning would improve the dish. Add a little and taste

again. Usually several tastings are needed before the seasoning is right.

Fresh herbs are becoming more widely available. When a fresh herb is not in season, however, you can use its dried form; substitute about 1 tablespoon of dried herb for every 3 tablespoons of fresh, chopped herb.

Many spices, especially ground pepper and grated nutmeg, are best when they are freshly prepared. Once these spices are ground, they quickly lose their aroma. It is therefore preferable to buy them whole and grind them as needed. Grind whole nutmeg with a special grinder, or grate it on the smallest holes of a grater.

Dried spices and herbs should be purchased in relatively small amounts because, after about six months, they lose a good deal of their zest. It is best to buy them gradually, as you need them for specific dishes, rather than to acquire them all at once in order to have a well-stocked kitchen.

In addition to herbs and spices, you can add zest to foods by using bottled flavorings such as mustard, vinegar, and soy sauce; aromatic vegetables such as onions, garlic, and carrots; citrus juices and rinds; ginger; and a variety of cheeses.

GETTING ORGANIZED

Good organization makes cooking much easier. First, of course, you must have all the ingredients. Prepare a shopping list to be sure you don't forget anything.

With care in menu planning, it's easy to serve even an elegant meal such as this one on a busy schedule. Country Watercress Soup (see page 24), Basic Chocolate Mousse (see page 123), and the Gratin of Potato Purée (see page 67) can be made ahead. The swordfish (see Grilled Fish Fillets With Mint Béarnaise Sauce, page 113) cooks quickly just before serving. For a lighter meal, serve a salad of sliced tomatoes with vinaigrette dressing instead of the potatoes.

Raspberry Sauce (see page 116) and a few garnishes turn a simple dessert of poached pears (see Poached Fruit in Syrup, page 118) into a spectacular one.

You can shop two or three days ahead, but remember that certain fragile ingredients, especially fish, shellfish, fresh herbs, and ground meat, are best used on the day purchased or the next day. Frozen meats and poultry, by contrast, may need a day or two to defrost properly. Tomatoes and some fruits are often sold underripe and will be at their best if left to ripen at room temperature for a few days. Seafood, meats, fine cheeses, and delicate produce will often be fresher and of better quality when purchased at specialty shops than at most supermarkets.

In cooking the dish, it is often easiest to clean and chop all the vegetables first. This depends on the dish, however. If, for example, the meat needs to cook for an hour before the vegetables are added, it is more efficient to prepare the vegetables while the meat is cooking.

EQUIPMENT

You don't need a huge, fully equipped kitchen to begin cooking. Some of the best dishes can be prepared with the simplest equipment.

If possible, try to purchase equipment of good quality. It is better to buy it little by little than to purchase poorly made equipment that will need to be replaced in a short time. The following is a description of the minimum equipment needed to begin cooking. As you continue cooking, you will gradually acquire more. Other types of equipment for specific uses are described in each chapter.

Cookware The best size for saucepans depends to a certain extent on whether you cook most often for one person or for six or more. Still, most kitchens should have at least one small saucepan (about 1 quart), two medium saucepans (about 2 quarts), and one large saucepan (about 3 or 4 quarts), as well as one large and one small frying pan. Cookware should be fairly heavy so that it heats evenly. The best-quality pans are generally quite expensive but give better results. Try to avoid saucepans of untreated aluminum because when wine or other acidic ingredients are put in them, both the ingredients and the pans discolor.

Knives Every kitchen should have at least four basic knives: a large chopping knife, a medium-sized slicing knife, a small paring knife, and a thin boning knife for delicate cutting.

A properly sharpened knife makes cutting work easier, more pleasant, and actually safer; many accidents are the result of pressing hard while trying to slice food with a dull knife. Have a sharpening steel on hand and use it often to keep the edge on your knives. In addition, have your knives professionally sharpened occasionally, about once every six months.

A good way to store knives is in or on a knife rack. If they are thrown into a drawer, their blades can become damaged.

Measuring Tools You need two types of measuring cups: a glass measuring cup, for liquids, and a set of metal or plastic measuring cups in which the ingredient measured can be leveled at the top, for dry ingredients. A set of standard measuring spoons is also essential. A scale, preferably with both American and metric weights, is useful.

Other Tools Other important utensils to have in the kitchen are a few wooden spoons; one or two small whisks; a ladle; a slotted spoon; a wide, slotted metal spatula; a grater; and a fairly large strainer. A relatively large cutting board that gives you room to work is also convenient.

A food processor makes chopping, slicing, and puréeing quick and easy and is definitely desirable in the kitchen. It can perform most of the functions of a blender and many of those of a mixer as well.

A FEW NOTES ON BASIC INGREDIENTS

Eggs Use large eggs unless otherwise specified.

Milk Use whole milk unless otherwise specified.

Butter and Margarine Unsalted, or "sweet," butter is of higher quality than salted, and should be used when it is specified. You can substitute margarine for butter, but the flavor of the final dish will not be as good.

Salad Oil Use any neutral-tasting vegetable oil, such as corn oil, safflower oil, sunflower seed oil, or peanut oil.

Flour Use all-purpose flour unless otherwise specified.

Wine Always use dry wine for cooking unless otherwise specified. The best wine is one that you also like to drink, but there is no need to use expensive wines for cooking. Do not use wine labeled "cooking wine" because salt has been added to it.

Citrus Rind When grating the rind of lemons, limes, or oranges, grate only the colored zest and not the underlying white pith, which is bitter.

BASIC MEASURES

Pinch = less than 1/8 teaspoon
1 tablespoon = 3 teaspoons
1/4 cup = 4 tablespoons
1/3 cup = 5 1/3 tablespoons
1/2 cup = 8 tablespoons
1 cup = 16 tablespoons
1 pint = 2 cups
1 quart = 4 cups
1 pound = 16 ounces

THE ART OF PRESENTATION

Presentation is the art of arranging the food on the plate or platter. Properly cooked food generally looks appetizing, but a little attention at serving time makes it look even better.

Whether to serve food on a platter or on plates is up to the cook. The choice usually depends on which way it is more convenient to serve. Some main courses, such as large roasts, are most impressive when arranged on a platter. To keep hot food warm, many cooks like to heat their plates and platters before serving.

Whether you use a platter or individual plates, the food will be most attractive if it is not crowded. If the food is of one color, a sprig of a fresh herb, a few cherry tomatoes, or a simple lemon garnish will add visual interest.

The step-by-step instructions here show how to cut lemons (or limes or oranges) for appealing decorative touches.

How to Make Zigzag Lemon Halves

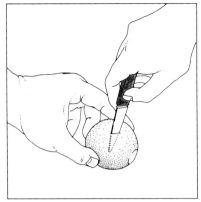

1. *Set the lemon on a board and cut off both ends to make flat surfaces. With one end facing you, use a paring knife to make a diagonal slit in the center, pushing the knife all the way through the lemon until the tip of the knife touches the board.*

2. *Turn the lemon slightly and make a second slit in the same way, joining the first at about a 90-degree angle.*

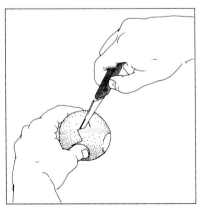

3. *Continue making slits in this manner, keeping the angle approximately the same, until you have made slits all around the lemon and it is cut in two. Be sure the last slit joins the first.*

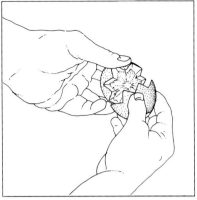

4. *Pull the halves apart. Set a parsley sprig in the center of each lemon half.*

How to Make Fluted Lemon Slices

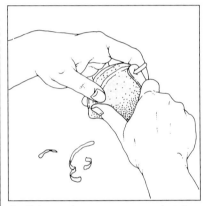

1. *Using a lemon zester, peel strips of lemon rind lengthwise at approximately equal intervals.*

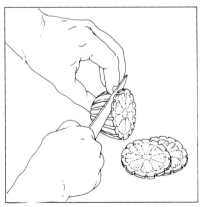

2. *Cut lemon in thin slices. For half slices, halve the lemon lengthwise, set it cut side down on a board, and slice it crosswise.*

BASIC TECHNIQUES OF FOOD PREPARATION

The five pages that follow contain directions for basic food-preparation techniques that are the beginning steps for many dishes. These techniques, for vegetables, seafood, and poultry, will be used often in the chapters that follow.

How to Use a Chopping Knife

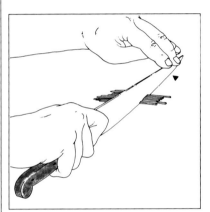

1. *Place the knife over the food to be chopped, with one hand holding the tip on the cutting surface and the other grasping the handle.*

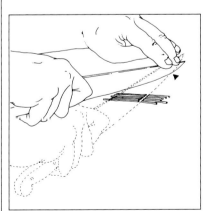

2. *With the curve of the knife as a pivot point never leaving the cutting surface, rock the knife down on the food and back up again. Repeat this up-and-down motion until the pieces are reduced to the desired size.*

How to Chop Fresh Herbs

The technique shown here is appropriate for all leafy herbs. Chives can be bunched and sliced thinly instead of chopped.

1. *Rinse the herb and dry thoroughly. Remove the leaves from the stems. Use a dry, large, heavy chopping knife and a dry board.*

2. *Use a chopping knife (see instructions at left) to mince the herb.*

TECHNIQUES FOR PREPARING VEGETABLES

How to Clean Leeks

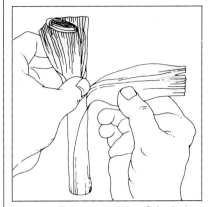

1. *Cut off the root ends of the leeks. Remove and discard the coarse outer layers; cut off and discard about 1 inch of the leek tops.*

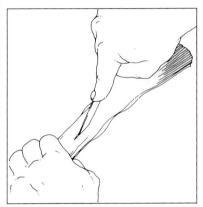

2. *Split each leek lengthwise twice, beginning about 1 inch from the root end and cutting toward the green end.*

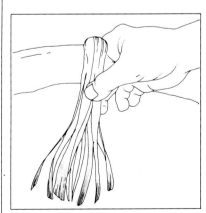

3. *Holding each leek by its root end, dip it several times in cold water. If dirt remains, soak in cold water for several minutes. Then separate the layers under running water to rinse away any clinging dirt. Drain.*

How to Slice an Onion

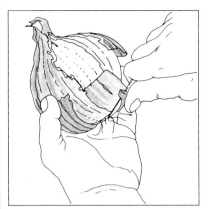

1. *With a paring knife, peel the onion.*

2. *To cut half slices, cut onion in half, top to bottom; lay it on cutting board, cut side down. Hold slicing knife in your cutting hand. Press the fingers of your other hand against the curved surface of the onion, with fingertips curled under; slice onion.*

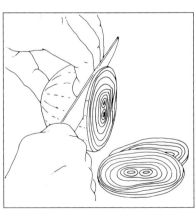

3. *To slice onion rounds (not half slices), it is easiest to use a food processor with a slicing blade. To slice them by hand, lay the peeled onion on its side and cut slices, using the fingertips to guide the knife.*

How to Chop an Onion

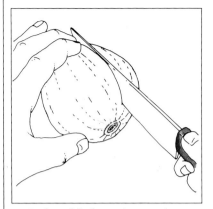

1. *Peel and halve onion as described for slicing; lay it cut side down on cutting board.*

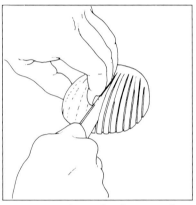

2. *Using a slicing knife, cut each onion half in vertical slices, starting nearly at the root end and slicing toward the stem end, but leaving the onion joined at its root end.*

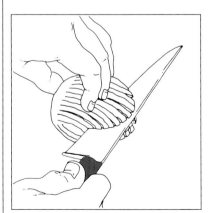

3. *Cut onion half in several horizontal slices, again leaving it attached at the root end.*

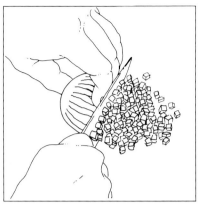

4. *Slice the onion crosswise from the stem end, forming tiny cubes.*

5. *Use a chopping knife (see page 11) to reduce the onion cubes to the desired size.*

Note Shallots are sliced and chopped in the same way onions are. Onions can also be sliced and chopped in a food processor. Follow the machine's instruction manual.

How to Peel, Seed, and Chop Tomatoes

How to Peel and Chop Garlic

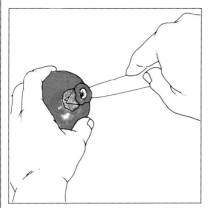

1. Use a paring knife to core the tomatoes.

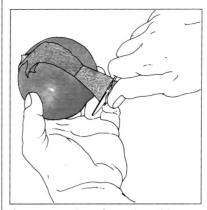

4. Remove them from the cold water and use a paring knife to pull off the skins.

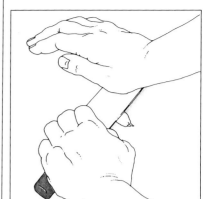

1. Put garlic clove on a board. Hold flat side of a large knife just above it. Lightly pound knife, hitting the garlic and loosening its skin. Pull skin off, cutting if necessary.

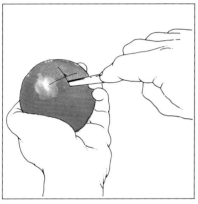

2. Turn tomatoes over and slit the skin in an X-shaped cut.

5. Halve the tomatoes horizontally with a chopping knife. Hold each half over a bowl, cut side down, and squeeze to remove the seeds.

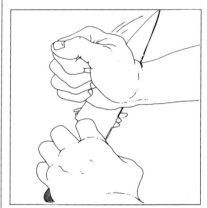

2. Return garlic to board and position knife above it as in step 1. Hit blade vigorously with side of fist to crush the garlic.

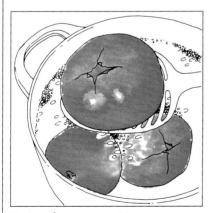

3. Put the tomatoes in a pan containing enough boiling water to cover them and boil for 15 seconds. Remove them with a slotted spoon and put them in a bowl of cold water. Leave for a few seconds.

6. Chop the tomatoes into small pieces.

3. To chop the garlic, cut it several times in one direction. Slice it against the direction of the first cuts. Use a chopping knife (see page 11) to mince the garlic.

MORE VEGETABLE PREPARATION TECHNIQUES

Cleaning Mushrooms Gently rinse mushrooms one at a time under cold running water; do not soak them in water. Dry mushrooms upside down on paper towels.

Peeling Potatoes Potatoes should be peeled unless otherwise stated. Peel potatoes with a vegetable peeler. With the sharp tip of the peeler, remove the "eyes" of each potato. If not using immediately, put the peeled potatoes in a bowl of cold water to prevent discoloring. Cut potatoes just before using unless otherwise instructed.

Peeling Baby Onions Bring a saucepan of water to a boil. Add onions and boil them 1 minute. Drain onions; rinse them with cold water until they are cool. Peel onions with paring knife.

Preparing Peppers Whether using sweet bell peppers or hot peppers, core them by cutting them in half and removing the stem, core, and seeds. Remove the white ribs inside the pepper. Wear rubber gloves when handling hot peppers. Wash the knives and cutting board immediately after cutting hot peppers.

Preparing Carrots Carrots should be peeled unless otherwise stated. Cut off carrot tops. Peel carrots using a vegetable peeler.

Cleaning Spinach Pull the spinach stems off the leaves; discard the stems. Swish the leaves around in a sinkful of cold water, lift them out into a bowl, and change the water in the sink. Repeat rinsing twice or until no sand remains.

Draining Cooked Vegetables Empty the contents of the saucepan into a strainer or colander so that all the water drains out.

TECHNIQUES FOR PREPARING SEAFOOD AND WHOLE POULTRY

How to Remove Skin From a Fish Fillet

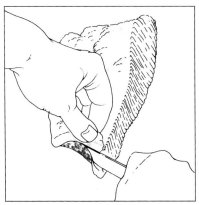

1. Use a flexible, thin-bladed boning knife. Set the fish fillet, skin side down, on a cutting board, with the thinner end of the fillet closest to you. Make a small cut between the skin and the meat of the fillet.

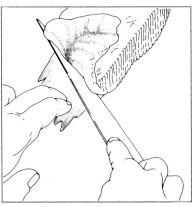

2. Holding the skin with one hand and the knife in the other, with the blade nearly parallel to the board, insert the knife where you made the cut. Move it away from you with a gentle sawing motion, at the same time pulling on the skin with your free hand. Continue until you free the skin from the flesh.

How to Remove Bones From a Fish Fillet

1. Run your fingers over the fish fillet to feel for bones. Usually the bones will be in a row.

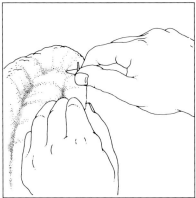

2. Remove any bones. You can gently pull them out with a pair of tweezers, a pastry crimper, or small pliers. Or you can do it with your fingers supplemented by a paring knife. Hold paring knife and grasp bone between knife and your thumb; pull the bone out. Do this carefully to avoid making large holes in the fillet.

How to Clean Mussels and Clams

Both mussels and clams must be cooked live.

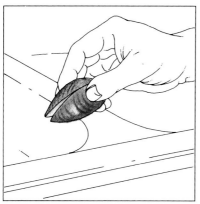

1. *Tap any open mussel or clam gently against the sink or another surface; it will close again if still alive. If a mussel or clam remains open after being tapped, discard it.*

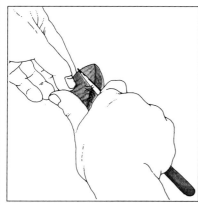

2. *Put the closed shellfish in a colander and rinse them well several times under cold running water. Scrub clams thoroughly with a stiff brush. Scrape mussels with a knife to remove the foreign particles that cling to them and the "beard" that joins them together. After mussels are cleaned, their shells should look bright and shiny.*

How to Shell and Devein Raw Shrimp

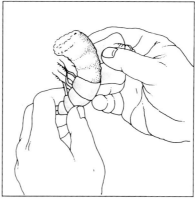

1. *Remove the rings of the shell from the shrimp one or two at a time, beginning at the wider end of the shrimp.*

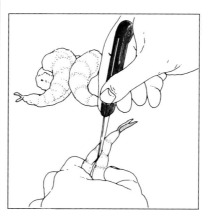

2. *Slit the shrimp down the whole length of the back with a paring knife.*

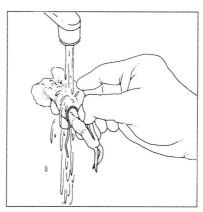

3. *Holding the shrimp under cold running water, use the knife tip to remove the long black "vein" (actually the shrimp's intestine).*

How to Prepare Whole Poultry for Roasting or Poaching

The following instructions are for whole poultry only; for directions on cutting up poultry, see page 91.

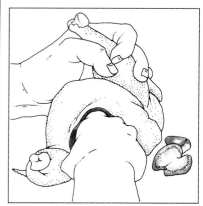

1. *Remove the neck and giblets from inside the bird; often they are in a bag.*

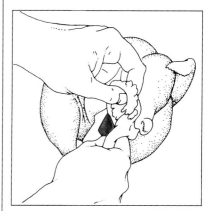

2. *If using a chicken, duck, or goose, pull out the fat from inside the bird on both sides near the tail.*

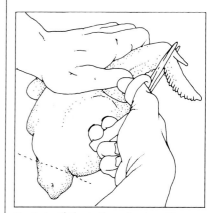

3. *Cut off the tail and wing tips. Save the neck, wing tips, and giblets (except the liver) for stock; reserve the liver for another use.*

15

Using a simple chicken stock and a few colorful additions, such as asparagus tips and mushrooms, you can easily prepare a light and lovely soup.

Stocks & Soups

Stock is one of the foundations of good cuisine. Slow cooking extracts flavor from meat, poultry, fish, or vegetables; this essence then gives a subtle but unmistakable richness to soups and sauces. This chapter discusses the technique of making your own homemade stock, and then helps you make the most of it in a wide range of superb soups, from Classic Beef Consommé (see page 23) to Minestrone With Pasta and Pesto (see page 30).

SOUP BASICS

The basic idea of a soup is extremely simple. The ingredients are covered with water and simmered gently. Gradually, they become tender and some of their essences seep slowly into the liquid, flavoring it. From these modest beginnings, countless soups have been developed, from hearty main-course soups and rich cream soups to clear consommés. Stocks, another product of slow simmering, are one of the foundations of good cuisine; they are special types of soup used to add flavor to many sauces and main dishes. Stocks are discussed in detail at right.

It is a common error to think that good soups can be made from old, tired ingredients. Although the components of soups do not all need to be crisp, fresh ingredients heighten the flavor of the soup. Freshness is especially important when the soup contains seafood, which must always be as fresh as possible for all uses. This does not mean, however, that leftovers have no place in soups. It's fine to add yesterday's cooked green beans, steamed rice, or roast chicken, for example, to a minestrone or other hearty soup. Frozen vegetables and diced meats can also be simmered in soups. It is important, however, to use at least some fresh ingredients to give the soup zest.

Good soups have a distinct character from one or a few main ingredients. This means it is not a good idea to add ingredients indiscriminately; the soup will turn into a hodgepodge of flavors.

Soup-making requires little equipment other than a large saucepan and a wooden spoon. An 8- or 12-quart stockpot and a large strainer, however, make stock preparation easier. For other soups, a heavy saucepan is desirable so that the ingredients will cook evenly. A food processor or blender is convenient for puréeing and chopping ingredients.

Serving

Soups can play several roles in a meal. A clear soup served in dainty bowls is an ideal beginning to an elegant dinner. A chunky soup, such as Minestrone With Pasta and Pesto (see page 30) or Spicy Beef Soup With Garbanzo Beans and Rice (see page 29), makes a warming lunch and is best served in larger bowls. Cream soups are so versatile that they can be served as a first course for almost any occasion; because they are rich, cream soups are best served in small bowls. Many soups, such as Country Watercress Soup (see page 24), are equally good hot or cold.

Soups can be brought to the table in beautiful tureens or ladled into bowls in the kitchen. Before serving hot soups, heat the tureen or bowls first. Serve cold soups in chilled bowls if you wish.

Making Soups Ahead

Most soups and all stocks can be prepared ahead, refrigerated or frozen, and reheated. Cool soups to room temperature before you refrigerate or freeze them; store them in covered containers.

Refrigerated soups should be reheated in a saucepan over medium-low heat. Cover chunky soups during reheating and do not stir too often so that the ingredients do not fall apart. Stir vegetable purée soups, cream soups, and velouté soups frequently during reheating to prevent scorching and sticking. It is best not to reheat soups containing egg yolks, however, because they may curdle. Soups containing thickeners such as flour, potatoes, or rice thicken on standing; when reheating the soup, stir in a few tablespoons of additional liquid if necessary. Many fresh herbs lose their flavor when reheated; if the herb is already in the soup, it is good to add a little more of it after reheating. When time allows, let frozen soups stand until they have defrosted before reheating them.

STOCKS

Stocks, which are sometimes called broths, add depth of flavor and aroma to dishes and play an important part in the best dishes of most cuisines. From Far Eastern to European cuisines, stock is the main ingredient of many sauces and soups made from meat, poultry, fish, and even vegetables. The flavor of the stock is the reason these dishes taste so rich and good. Stocks also add flavor to ingredients as they cook, especially during poaching, braising, and stewing. Although the contribution of stock is subtle, it gives an unmistakable richness to dishes. Beef stock has the deepest flavor and color, followed by chicken stock; fish stock is the lightest.

Stock is economical to prepare because its ingredients are often free or cost very little. The main ingredients of stock are soup bones and water. Beef and veal bones are available from butcher shops and at many supermarkets. Chicken wings or necks for chicken stock are found in almost every supermarket. Fish bones for fish stock can be obtained at fish markets.

Because stock is a base for many different dishes, it should have a relatively neutral taste flavored mainly by the meat, poultry, or fish. Additional flavors might clash with the taste of the ingredients added later when the stock is used in soups or sauces. Aromatic vegetables, such as onions and carrots; herbs, such as thyme and bay leaves; and peppercorns are often added to the stock base. Salt is not added because the stock might be used in a dish that already contains salty ingredients. In addition, if the stock is reduced to concentrate its flavor, it can become too salty if the salt is added at the beginning. Instead, the dishes using the stock are seasoned to taste.

Many of the most attractive soups and sauces are based on clear stocks (see pages 20–21). To keep stocks clear, skim the foam and fat that collects on top; if the stock is not skimmed frequently, the fat and foam cook into the stock and make it cloudy or muddy. An especially clear stock results if the ingredients simmer uncovered. This is practical for fish stock, which is ready after only 20 minutes of simmering, but less so for the others, because the liquid evaporates rapidly and water needs to be added frequently. A compromise is to cover the stock partially as it simmers so that steam can escape but the liquid does not evaporate too quickly.

Although meat stocks require long cooking to extract the good flavor from the bones, they are easy to prepare and require almost no attention as they simmer. It is easy to keep stock on hand by making it in large quantities and freezing it in relatively small containers.

The cook who is in a great hurry can substitute canned broths or bouillon cubes for beef and chicken stocks, and bottled clam juice for fish stock. However, these are often excessively salty and will never give the same taste as a homemade stock, which has the freshest, most natural flavor and is free of preservatives. Commercial stocks are not suitable for clear or delicate soups because these depend on excellent stock for their flavor.

Special Feature

SIMPLE SOUP GARNISHES

Garnishes put the finishing touch on a soup. When preparing smooth, creamy soups, cooks often reserve a small amount of the main ingredient for garnish before puréeing it with the rest of the soup. Chopped fresh herbs also add color and a lively flavor to most soups. A bowl of grated cheese is a popular accompaniment for many vegetable soups. However, if the soup contains a variety of colorful ingredients, it may not require any garnish.

Purée, cream, and velouté soups can be garnished with croutons. Their crunchy texture provides a pleasant contrast to the smoothness of the soup. To prevent the croutons from becoming soggy, serve them in a separate dish rather than in the soup tureen, letting each person add some to the soup at the last minute.

Sautéed Croutons are a good accompaniment to all smooth vegetable soups and velouté soups. Baked Cheese Croutons are best with those vegetable soups that go well with cheese, such as Country Watercress Soup (page 24) and Mushroom Soup With Chives (page 26).

SAUTÉED CROUTONS

4 slices white bread
4 to 6 tablespoons salad oil

1. Cut crust from bread. Cut bread slices in pieces about ½ inch square.

2. Heat 4 tablespoons oil in a large, heavy frying pan. Test oil by adding a bread square; when oil is hot enough, it will bubble vigorously around bread. Remove bread piece with slotted spatula.

3. To hot oil, add enough remaining bread squares to make one layer in frying pan. Toss them frequently, or turn them with a slotted spatula, so that they will brown evenly on all sides. Fry the squares until they are golden brown.

4. Transfer fried bread squares to a strainer and drain them. Then transfer to paper towels to drain further. If pan is dry, add remaining 2 tablespoons oil and heat thoroughly. Fry remaining bread squares as before. Croutons can be made 2 hours ahead; they should be served at room temperature.

Serves about 4.

BAKED CHEESE CROUTONS

4 slices white bread
2 tablespoons butter, softened
3 tablespoons grated Parmesan cheese

1. Preheat oven to 400° F. Generously butter a baking sheet.

2. Cut crust from bread. Spread bread with butter and sprinkle with cheese. Cut each slice in pieces about ½ inch square and transfer to buttered baking sheet.

3. Bake until cheese melts and bread becomes crisp (about 7 minutes). Serve hot.

Serves about 4.

... ON SOUP

- *Green tops of leeks can be added to any stock to add flavor. The leeks should be thoroughly cleaned first (see pages 11).*

- *Small pieces of onion, carrot, and celery can be frozen in bags or containers and saved for stock. However, do not add all sorts of leftover vegetables to stocks because many will add undesirably strong flavors.*

- *If you wish to substitute canned broth for homemade stock, use a regular-strength broth; the quantity remains the same.*

- *If a soup is too thick, stir in a little more of its main liquid—usually stock, milk, cream, or water.*

- *If a soup is too thin, boil it, uncovered, to evaporate the excess liquid. However, if the soup contains chunks of meat, fish, or other ingredients that are already fully cooked, remove them with a slotted spoon before boiling so that they will not fall apart.*

- *Soups containing purées or flour should be stirred during cooking or reheating to prevent sticking.*

- *If you must reheat velouté soups containing egg yolks, do so very carefully in a double boiler over simmering water and stir the soup constantly. It should not boil.*

- *Soups that will be served cold require more seasoning than those served hot. Taste them for flavor after they are chilled rather than before.*

- *When storing stocks or soups for freezing, do not fill containers to the top because the liquid expands as it freezes.*

Handling Stock

Cooling Stock Stock should be cooled quickly so that it can be refrigerated or frozen as soon as possible. If left too long in a warm kitchen, stock can spoil.

To cool stock quickly, put bowls of strained stock in the sink and fill the sink with enough cold water to come almost to the rim of the bowls. To speed the cooling, add ice cubes to the water in the sink. Change the water when it becomes warm.

When the stock is lukewarm, it can be refrigerated in the bowl or poured into 1- or 2-cup containers, covered, labeled, and frozen. Meat stocks can be frozen about 6 months; fish stocks for about 3 months.

Removing Fat From Stock Before the stock is used, the fat should be removed so the stock will be clear and will not taste greasy. Even if meat and chicken stock are skimmed often while they simmer, quite a bit of fat remains. (Fish stock contains very little fat.)

The easiest way to remove the fat is to refrigerate the stock. As it cools, the fat solidifies on the surface, and it can be scraped off with a spoon.

To remove fat from hot stock, skim the fat from the surface with a spoon. Then draw strips of paper towels across the surface to remove the last bits of fat.

Defrosting Stock Stock frozen in a plastic container can be defrosted quickly by the following method: Set the container, uncovered, in a pan of hot water for a few minutes until the stock at the edges and bottom defrosts. Then push on the bottom of the container and slip the frozen stock into a saucepan.

Cover the saucepan and heat the stock over medium-low heat until it melts and can be measured. Measure the desired amount. Place the remaining stock in a container and freeze it immediately.

CHICKEN STOCK

Chicken stock, the most versatile stock of all, is the base of a great variety of soups and sauces. Its wonderful home-cooked flavor makes it a standby in both Oriental and Western cuisines.

The stock is best after 3 hours of simmering but already has a good flavor after 2 hours. Whenever you buy a chicken, you can save the giblets (except the liver, which has too strong a flavor), wing tips, or other trimmings in the freezer and add them to other chicken parts when making stock. Do not use the giblets alone, however, because the flavor of the stock will be less delicate.

> 3 pounds chicken wings, chicken backs, or a mixture of wings, backs, necks, and giblets (except livers)
> 2 medium onions, peeled and quartered
> 2 medium carrots, peeled and quartered
> 2 bay leaves
> 10 stems parsley (without leaves)
> ½ teaspoon black peppercorns
> About 16 cups water
> ½ teaspoon dried thyme

1. Combine chicken, onions, carrots, bay leaves, parsley, and peppercorns in a stockpot, kettle, or other large pot. Add enough water to cover the ingredients. Bring to a boil, skimming foam that collects on top. Stir in thyme.

2. Reduce heat to very low so that stock bubbles very gently. Partially cover and cook, skimming foam and fat occasionally, for at least 2 or up to 3 hours.

3. Strain stock into large bowls, discarding solids. If stock is not to be used immediately, cool to lukewarm. Refrigerate in the bowls until cold and remove fat from the surface. The stock can be stored, covered, in the refrigerator for 3 days, or frozen.

Makes about 10 cups.

BEEF STOCK

Use beef stock in meat dishes: brown sauces served with meat, meat stews, and meat soups. Beef stock also enlivens vegetable soups, such as minestrone, that do not contain cream or milk. Brown veal stock, which has a more delicate flavor and a more gelatinous texture than beef stock, can be used interchangeably with beef stock. Many cooks prefer veal stock because it helps to thicken soups and sauces naturally. (See variation at right.)

The bones and vegetables in this recipe are first roasted to give the stock a brown color and rich flavor. For the best flavor, use knuckle bones with some meat attached.

>   4   *pounds beef soup bones,*
>   *chopped in a few pieces by*
>   *the butcher*
>   2   *medium onions, unpeeled,*
>   *root end cut off, quartered*
>   2   *medium carrots, scrubbed but*
>   *not peeled, quartered*
>   2   *stalks celery, cut in*
>   *about 2-inch pieces*
>   2   *bay leaves*
>   10 *stems parsley (without leaves)*
>   4   *cloves garlic, unpeeled*
>   ½   *teaspoon black peppercorns*
>   *About 16 cups water*
>   ½   *teaspoon dried thyme*

1. Preheat oven to 450° F. Put bones in a roasting pan and roast them, turning them over occasionally with a slotted metal spatula, until they begin to brown (about 30 minutes). Add onions, carrots, and celery and roast them until browned (about 30 minutes).

2. Using a slotted spatula, transfer bones and vegetables to a stockpot, kettle, or other large pot; do not add fat from roasting pan. To ingredients in stockpot, add bay leaves, parsley, garlic, peppercorns, and enough water to cover. Bring to a boil, skimming foam that collects on top. Stir in thyme.

3. Reduce heat to very low so that stock bubbles very gently. Partially cover and cook, skimming foam and fat occasionally, for at least 4 or up to 6 hours. During first 2 hours of cooking, add hot water occasionally to keep ingredients covered.

4. Strain stock into large bowls, discarding bones and vegetables. If not using immediately, cool to lukewarm. Refrigerate until cold and remove fat from surface. Stock can be stored, covered, in the refrigerator for 3 days, or frozen.

Makes about 8 cups.

Brown Veal Stock Substitute veal bones, preferably knuckle bones, for the beef bones.

FISH STOCK

Fish stock is the basis for many fish and shellfish soups and sauces. When you purchase fish at a fish market, ask for fish bones. Often, they are free. Tell the fishmonger you want them for fish stock so that you will receive suitable bones. The best bones come from mild fish, such as sea bass and halibut. Do not use bones from strong-flavored fish, such as tuna or mackerel. If bones are not available, you can substitute 1½ pounds of fish pieces for chowder.

>   2   *pounds fish bones, tails,*
>   *and heads*
>   1   *tablespoon unsalted butter*
>   1   *medium onion, sliced*
>   ½   *cup dry white wine*
>   7½ *cups water*
>   1   *bay leaf*
>   8   *stems parsley (without leaves)*
>   ½   *teaspoon dried thyme*

1. Put fish bones in bowl in sink. Let cold water run over bones for 5 minutes.

2. Melt butter in stockpot, kettle, or large saucepan over low heat. Add onion and cook, stirring often, until soft but not brown (about 10 minutes).

3. Add fish bones, wine, water, bay leaf, and parsley. Mix well. Bring to a boil and skim thoroughly to remove foam. Stir in thyme. Reduce heat to low and simmer uncovered, skimming occasionally, for 20 minutes.

4. Strain through fine strainer into large bowl, discarding solids.

5. If not using immediately, cool to room temperature. Pour into 1- or 2-cup containers. Refrigerate, covered, up to 2 days or freeze up to 3 months.

Makes about 6 cups.

CLEAR SOUPS

Just a little seasoning and a few tablespoons of a chopped fresh herb are enough to turn a good stock into a refreshing, clear soup. Clear soups can contain a few simple additions as well. These soups are low in calories because thoroughly skimmed stock is virtually free of fat.

Consommé is the most refined and probably the most highly regarded of clear soups. Because consommé must be sparkling clear, a special clarification procedure is followed to prepare it. In this rather unusual technique, egg whites and flavoring ingredients are whisked with stock over heat. At first, paradoxically, the whites make the stock extremely cloudy. As the egg whites cook, however, they form a filter that gradually traps the particles suspended in the stock. When the stock is strained, the consommé is clear and richly flavored.

Clear soups are often flavored with fortified wines, such as Madeira and sherry, and garnished with cooked vegetables, rice, or soup pasta. Most vegetables can be cooked in the soup, but rice or pasta should be cooked separately so that their starch will not cloud the soup. Stir the cooked rice or pasta into the hot soup at the last minute. Any addition to consommé, however, should be cooked separately to ensure the soup's perfect clarity.

Vegetables such as carrots, leeks, and celery cut in julienne, or very thin strips, are a classic garnish for this Madeira-flavored Beef Consommé (opposite page) and other clear soups.

CHICKEN SOUP WITH CARROTS AND DILL

This is an easy way to transform simple chicken stock into a versatile first course. Practically any entrée, from roasts to creamy stews and spicy dishes, can follow it. Remember that dill is a fragile herb and should be used within two days of purchase.

> 5 cups Chicken Stock (see page 20)
> 3 medium carrots, peeled and cut in thin slices
> 2 small stalks celery, including leafy tops
> 5 sprigs fresh dill
>   Salt and pepper
> 1 tablespoon snipped fresh dill

1. Skim any fat from surface of stock. Combine stock, carrots, celery stalks, dill sprigs, and a pinch of salt and pepper in a large saucepan and bring to a boil.

2. Reduce heat to low. Cover and simmer, skimming foam occasionally, until carrots are tender (about 30 minutes). Discard celery and dill sprigs. Soup can be kept, covered, up to 2 days in refrigerator.

3. Reheat soup if necessary. Stir in snipped dill. Taste and add more salt and pepper, if needed. Serve hot.

Serves 4.

CLASSIC BEEF CONSOMMÉ WITH VEGETABLE JULIENNE AND MADEIRA

Consommé is a light first course with a concentrated beef flavor. It is made from beef stock, which is clarified by simmering with egg whites. Ground beef and chopped vegetables cook in the stock together with the whites and give the soup its rich flavor. Preparing consommé does demand patience because quite a bit of whisking is required at the beginning of the clarification process.

Adding a julienne of vegetables to consommé is only one way to garnish this basic soup recipe. Almost any delicate vegetable in season, such as peas or zucchini, can be added instead. The vegetables are cooked separately so they will not cloud the consommé. Other suitable additions are cooked rice, pasta, chopped fresh herbs, and diced raw tomatoes.

> 1 small leek
> 4 cups Beef Stock (see page 21)
> Salt and pepper
> 3 egg whites
> ½ pound very lean ground beef
> 1 medium carrot, quartered lengthwise and cut in thin slices
> 1 medium stalk celery, halved lengthwise and cut in thin slices
> 2 medium tomatoes, cored and diced
> ¼ cup Madeira

Vegetable Julienne

> 1 small stalk celery
> Reserved white and light green part of leek (see step 1)
> 1 small carrot
> 1¼ cups Beef Stock (see page 21)
> Salt and pepper

1. Prepare and clean leek (see page 11). Use dark green part of leek for making consommé and cut it in thin slices; reserve white and light green part for vegetable julienne.

2. Skim fat thoroughly from surface of stock. Heat stock until warm in large, heavy saucepan. Remove from heat and remove any remaining fat by quickly drawing strips of paper towel over surface. Season stock to taste with salt and pepper.

3. Whisk egg whites lightly in a large bowl until foamy. Add leek, beef, carrot, celery, and tomatoes and mix thoroughly with egg whites. Slowly ladle in about 2 cups stock, stirring well after each addition. Slowly pour in remaining stock and mix well. Return to saucepan.

4. Cook mixture over medium heat, using large whisk to stir constantly. Stop whisking as soon as mixture just begins to bubble and looks milky; mixture should reach about 180° F on a thermometer. Continue cooking 1 or 2 more minutes, until a foamy crust forms on surface of soup, indicating that filter of egg whites has risen to top.

5. Reduce heat to low. Using ladle, make small hole in egg white filter near side of pan so that soup bubbles mainly in hole. Cook, uncovered, 30 minutes without stirring mixture or moving saucepan. Remove from heat. Taste liquid for seasoning, adding more salt and pepper through hole if necessary, but do not stir.

6. Line a large strainer with several layers of dampened, wrung-out cheesecloth. Set strainer above a medium saucepan, leaving room for consommé to drip through into saucepan without coming in contact with strainer. Slowly and carefully begin to ladle consommé into strainer, beginning where hole was made.

When most of consommé is ladled through, carefully slide egg white filter and remaining consommé into strainer. Let consommé drip through but do not press on filter. If consommé is not very clear, strain it again through mixture in cheesecloth. Discard solids in cheesecloth.

7. Remove any remaining fat by quickly drawing strips of paper towel over surface of consommé. Soup can be prepared ahead up to this point and kept, covered, up to 2 days in refrigerator.

8. Prepare Vegetable Julienne.

9. Bring consommé nearly to a boil and stir in julienne and Madeira. Serve hot, in small soup bowls.

Serves 3 or 4.

Vegetable Julienne Peel celery, using a vegetable peeler, to remove strings. Cut celery, reserved white and light green part of leek, and carrot into pieces about 1½ inches long. Cut carrot pieces lengthwise into slices ⅛ inch thick, then cut each piece again lengthwise at ⅛-inch intervals to make thin strips. Cut celery and leeks into thin lengthwise strips about same size as carrot strips. Put vegetable strips in medium saucepan and add beef stock and a small pinch of salt and pepper. Bring to a boil and skim off any foam. Reduce heat to low, cover, and simmer until tender (about 8 minutes). Drain vegetables thoroughly, reserving cooking liquid. (Cooking liquid can be reused as stock. Do not add it to consommé, or consommé will cloud.)

VEGETABLE PURÉE SOUPS

Purée soups are very quick and easy to prepare, and many of them are delicious hot or cold. Puréed vegetables give these soups both their characteristic flavor and their thickness. The vegetables are first cooked in stock or water and then puréed with their cooking liquid. Vegetables with a relatively high starch content are sufficient to thicken the soup. Most vegetables, however, cannot thicken the soup alone, and a small amount of rice or potatoes is added to give the soup body. Almost any fresh herb enhances the flavor of these soups. Some cooks further enrich purée soups with a little cream or unsalted butter just before they are served.

The vegetables can be puréed in a food processor, a blender, or a food mill. Using a blender or food processor is the easiest method and produces the smoothest soups. To purée a soup in a food processor, add the solids and a few tablespoons of the liquid. To make a purée in a blender, add all the liquid along with the cooked vegetables. A food mill is useful for puréeing fibrous vegetables such as celery or watercress because the strings do not go through the mill. Another way to eliminate strings is to purée the soup in a blender or food processor and then strain it.

CREAMY SQUASH SOUP WITH SAUTÉED GREEN VEGETABLES

Bright green vegetables provide a contrast of color and texture to this smooth, bright orange soup. Note that the recipe can be prepared through step 2 and then stored in the refrigerator up to 2 days before it is completed and served.

> 2 pounds winter squash, such as banana squash
> 1½ cups water
> 1 cup milk
> Salt and white pepper
> 1 tablespoon butter

Green Vegetable Garnish

> ½ cup shelled fresh peas (½ lb unshelled) or frozen green peas
> 2 green onions
> 2 tablespoons butter
> 2 leaves of butter lettuce, cut in thin strips
> Salt and pepper

1. Cut squash in pieces and cut off peel. Remove any seeds or stringy flesh. Cut squash flesh in cubes. Put in a medium saucepan with the water and a pinch of salt. Cover and bring to a boil. Reduce heat to low and simmer, stirring often, until tender (about 20 minutes).

2. Purée squash flesh in a food processor, blender, or food mill. Return purée to saucepan of cooking liquid. Bring to a boil, reduce heat to low, and simmer, uncovered, stirring often, for 5 minutes. Add milk and bring to a simmer. Cook over low heat, stirring often, 5 minutes. Season to taste with salt and pepper. Soup can be prepared ahead up to this point and kept, covered, up to 2 days in refrigerator.

3. Prepare Green Vegetable Garnish.

4. Reheat soup, if necessary, over medium-low heat, stirring. Remove hot soup from heat and stir in butter. Ladle soup into bowls and top each with some Green Vegetable Garnish.

Serves 4.

Green Vegetable Garnish

1. If using fresh peas, add them to a medium saucepan of boiling salted water and cook, uncovered, over high heat until just tender (about 5 minutes). Drain well. If using frozen peas, defrost them.

2. Keep white and green parts of green onions separate. Cut white part in thin slices. Slice enough of green part to obtain 1 tablespoon.

3. Melt butter in a medium frying pan and stir in white part of green onions. Cover and cook over low heat, stirring occasionally, until tender (about 5 minutes). Add lettuce and peas and cook just until lettuce wilts and peas are hot. Stir in reserved tablespoon of green part of green onions. Season mixture lightly with salt and pepper.

COUNTRY WATERCRESS SOUP

This creamy soup, which can be served hot or cold, is lightly thickened with potato. Serve the soup hot with Baked Cheese Croutons (see page 19) or cold with French bread. This soup thickens as it chills. If it becomes too thick, gradually stir in another 2 to 3 tablespoons of cream or milk just before serving.

> 2 medium leeks
> 2 bunches watercress (10 oz total)
> 1 medium potato
> 2 tablespoons butter
> 1 medium onion, sliced
> 1½ cups Chicken Stock (see page 20)
> Salt and white pepper
> 1½ cups milk
> ¼ to ½ cup whipping cream
> Freshly grated nutmeg

1. Wash and trim leeks (see page 11). Cut white and light green parts of leeks in thin slices; reserve dark green part for other uses.

2. Thoroughly rinse watercress, discard large stems, and reserve only upper, leafy third of each bunch. Reserve 8 to 12 attractive watercress leaves for garnish. Plunge bunches of watercress into large saucepan of boiling water. Bring back to a boil, drain immediately, and rinse under cold running water. Drain thoroughly and squeeze dry.

3. Peel potato and cut in thin slices.

4. Melt butter in heavy saucepan over low heat. Add onion and leeks and cook, stirring often, until soft but not brown (about 10 minutes). Add watercress bunches and cook, stirring, for 2 minutes. Add potato, stock, and a pinch of salt and pepper and bring to a boil. Reduce heat to low, cover, and simmer, stirring occasionally, until potatoes are tender (about 20 minutes).

5. Purée soup through a food mill. Alternatively, purée it in a blender or food processor, then strain to remove stringy parts of watercress.

6. Return soup to saucepan and add milk. Bring to a boil, stirring occasionally. Add ¼ cup cream and bring again to a boil. If soup is too thick, stir in remaining ¼ cup cream. Add nutmeg. Taste and add salt and pepper, if needed.

7. Prepare garnish by dipping a small strainer containing reserved watercress leaves into small saucepan of boiling water for ½ minute. Rinse and drain.

8. Serve soup hot or cold. To chill hot soup, cool slightly, then cover and refrigerate until thoroughly cold (several hours or overnight). Ladle soup into bowls and garnish with blanched watercress leaves.

Serves 4.

Smooth Carrot Soup With Croutons (see page 26) is a warming first course for winter meals. It is colorful, satisfying, and easy to prepare with the aid of a food processor or blender.

25

SMOOTH CARROT SOUP WITH CROUTONS

This golden orange soup, lightly thickened with rice, combines the sweet, delicate flavor of carrots with the rich taste of chicken stock.

- ¼ cup butter
  White part of 2 green onions, finely chopped
- 1¼ pounds carrots (5 large), finely diced
- 2½ cups Chicken Stock (see page 20)
- 3 tablespoons medium- or long-grain rice
  Salt and pepper
  Pinch of sugar
- ¾ to 1 cup milk
  Sautéed Croutons (see page 19)

1. In medium-sized, heavy saucepan, melt 2 tablespoons butter. Add onion and carrots; cook over low heat, stirring often, until softened (about 10 minutes).

2. Add stock, rice, salt, pepper, and sugar to saucepan and bring to a boil. Reduce heat to low, cover, and cook until carrots and rice are very tender (about 30 minutes).

3. Using slotted spoon, transfer carrots and rice to a food processor, reserving their cooking liquid. Purée carrots until fine. With motor running, gradually pour in carrot cooking liquid. Purée until very smooth *Or:* Transfer carrots and rice to a blender along with their cooking liquid; purée until smooth.

4. Return soup to saucepan. Simmer, uncovered, over low heat, stirring often, for 5 minutes.

5. Add ¾ cup milk and bring soup to a boil, stirring. If soup is too thick, stir in remaining milk. Taste for seasoning. Soup can be kept, covered, up to 2 days in refrigerator.

6. If necessary, reheat soup over medium-low heat, stirring. Stir in remaining 2 tablespoons butter. Ladle soup into bowls; serve croutons separately.

Serves 4.

CREAM SOUPS AND VELOUTÉ SOUPS

These classic soups can be made from vegetables, seafood, or poultry and are ideal first courses for festive dinners. Like Cream Sauce (see page 36) and Velouté Sauce (see page 38), these soups acquire body and a smooth, silky texture from a roux of butter and flour cooked together. The two types of soup gain their distinctive flavors from the ingredients added to the roux. In cream soups, milk is added to the roux; in velouté soups a light-colored stock, usually fish stock or chicken stock, is added. When the main ingredient of these soups is a vegetable, it often is puréed as in vegetable purée soups (see section starting on page 24). These soups can contain pieces of small fish, shellfish, chicken, and certain vegetables. Bisque is a special type of shellfish-flavored velouté soup.

Both cream soups and veloutés are usually enriched with cream. Velouté soups are often further enriched with egg yolks, which impart a velvety smoothness (velouté means "velvety" in French). If you want to prepare velouté soups ahead and reheat them, add the egg yolks after the soup is reheated.

Because both these soups contain flour, it is especially important to cook them in a heavy saucepan, which prevents the flour from sticking and burning. A whisk is most practical for stirring soups that do not contain any chunks; otherwise, a wooden spoon is best. Stir often, moving the whisk or spoon over the entire surface of the saucepan and around the edges. This prevents the flour from forming lumps.

MUSHROOM SOUP WITH CHIVES

Mushrooms give this soup a deep, full flavor that makes the addition of stock unnecessary. All this soup needs for accompaniment is some French or sourdough bread. Follow this rich, creamy first course with a simple entrée, such as roast chicken or grilled fish or steaks.

- 3 tablespoons butter
- 2 medium shallots, minced
- ¾ pound mushrooms, halved and thinly sliced
- 3 tablespoons flour
- 3 cups milk
- ¾ cup whipping cream
- 4 teaspoons thinly sliced chives
  Salt and white pepper

1. Melt butter in a large, heavy saucepan over medium heat. Stir in shallots and cook 1 minute. Stir in mushrooms, cover, and cook, shaking pan occasionally, until mushrooms are tender (about 5 minutes). Uncover and cook over medium-high heat until liquid produced by mushrooms evaporates.

2. Reduce heat to low. Stir in flour and cook, stirring constantly, until mixture is well blended and bubbly (about 3 minutes).

3. Remove from heat. Gradually pour milk into mushroom mixture, stirring and scraping bottom of saucepan thoroughly. Bring to a boil over medium-high heat, stirring constantly. Stir in cream and bring to a simmer, stirring. Reduce heat to low and simmer soup, uncovered, stirring often, until thickened to taste (about 10 minutes).

4. Stir in 3 teaspoons of the chives. Taste and add salt and pepper, if needed. Serve hot, sprinkled with remaining chives.

Serves 4.

FISH VELOUTÉ SOUP WITH FRESH HERBS

This classic soup demonstrates how fish stock can be made quickly into a delicious first course with the addition of a few fresh flavorings. For a special touch, you can enrich this basic velouté soup with shellfish. For example, cook a few small shrimp or scallops in the fish stock, remove them, and add them to the finished soup with the herbs. The soup can be prepared through step 3, then stored in the refrigerator up to a day before it is completed and served.

> 2 medium leeks
> ¼ cup butter
> 3 tablespoons flour
> 3 cups Fish Stock (see page 21)
>   Salt and pepper
> 3 egg yolks
> ⅔ cup whipping cream
> 1 tablespoon chopped fresh tarragon
> 1 tablespoon thinly sliced chives
> 1 tablespoon chopped parsley

1. Wash and trim leeks (see page 11). Finely chop white part of leeks; reserve green part for other uses.

2. Melt butter in a medium-sized, heavy saucepan over low heat. Add leeks and cook, stirring, until soft (about 5 minutes). Whisk in flour. Cook over low heat, whisking constantly, until mixture turns a light beige color (about 3 minutes). Remove from heat.

3. Gradually ladle fish stock into flour mixture, whisking. Bring to a boil over medium-high heat, whisking constantly. Add a small pinch of salt and pepper. Reduce heat to medium-low and simmer soup, uncovered, whisking often, for 5 minutes. Soup can be prepared ahead up to this point and kept, covered, up to 1 day in refrigerator.

4. Bring soup to simmer in a medium-sized, heavy saucepan over medium-low heat, whisking. Remove from heat. Whisk egg yolks and cream in a medium bowl until blended. Gradually whisk in about 1 cup of the hot soup. Whisk this mixture into soup remaining in saucepan. Cook over low heat, whisking constantly, until soup thickens slightly (about 3 minutes); do not boil. Remove from heat.

5. Stir in tarragon, chives, and parsley. Taste and add more salt and pepper, if needed. Serve hot.

Serves 4.

CHICKEN AND CUCUMBER VELOUTÉ SOUP

Cucumbers are not only for salads. This soup gains extra body from a purée of lightly cooked cucumbers, which add an intriguing flavor to the chicken stock. The soup is garnished with diced cucumber and rice. This recipe can be prepared up to a day ahead through step 7, then stored in the refrigerator before it is completed and served.

> ¼ cup long-grain rice
> 1½ cups boiling salted water
> 5 tablespoons butter
> 3 tablespoons flour
> 3½ cups Chicken Stock (see page 20)
>   Salt and white pepper
> 3 medium cucumbers (1½ lbs total), peeled
> ⅔ cup whipping cream
>   Pinch of cayenne pepper
> 1 tablespoon chopped parsley, for garnish

1. Cook rice in boiling water in a medium saucepan over medium-high heat until just tender (about 14 minutes). Drain thoroughly and reserve for garnish.

2. Melt 3 tablespoons of the butter in a medium-sized, heavy saucepan over low heat. Whisk in flour. Cook over low heat, whisking constantly, until mixture turns a light beige color (2 to 3 minutes). Remove from heat.

3. Gradually ladle 3 cups of the stock into flour mixture, whisking. Bring to a boil, whisking constantly, over medium-high heat. Add a pinch of salt and white pepper. Reduce heat to medium-low and simmer, uncovered, whisking often, for 5 minutes.

4. Halve 2 of the cucumbers and remove seeds. Cut in thin slices. Melt remaining 2 tablespoons of butter in a medium frying pan over low heat and stir in cucumber slices. Cover and cook, stirring occasionally, until softened (about 5 minutes). Add remaining ½ cup chicken stock, cover, and bring to a simmer. Reduce heat to low and cook until cucumbers are very tender (about 5 minutes).

5. Transfer cucumbers and liquid to a blender or food processor. Purée until very smooth (about 2 minutes). Add to soup and simmer, uncovered, over medium heat, stirring often, for 5 minutes.

6. Stir in cream and bring to a boil. Add cayenne. Simmer, stirring, until soup thickens to taste (about 2 minutes). Taste and add more salt and white pepper if needed.

7. Halve remaining cucumber, remove seeds, and cut in small dice. Add dice to a medium saucepan of boiling salted water and boil, uncovered, until just tender (about 3 minutes). Soup can be prepared ahead up to this point and kept, covered, up to 1 day in refrigerator; refrigerate cucumber dice and rice in separate containers.

8. Reheat soup, if necessary, over medium-low heat, stirring. To reheat cucumber dice, put them in a pan of boiling water and heat ½ minute; drain well.

9. Stir rice into hot soup and heat briefly. Ladle soup into shallow bowls and garnish with diced cucumber and chopped parsley.

Serves 4.

Shrimp Bisque gets its wonderful seafood flavor from a rich base made by simmering shrimp and shells in fish stock. Whole shrimp, cooked directly in the finished soup, impart additional shellfish flavor.

SHRIMP BISQUE

Serve this soup as the first course of an extra-special dinner. It can be prepared up to a day ahead through step 7, then stored in the refrigerator until it is completed and served.

1¼ *pounds small or medium-sized raw, unshelled shrimp, rinsed*
 6 *tablespoons butter*
   Half a medium onion, chopped
 1 *small carrot, chopped*
 ½ *cup dry white wine*
 2 *tablespoons brandy*
 3 *cups Fish Stock (see page 21)*
   Salt and pepper
 3 *tablespoons flour*
 2 *teaspoons tomato paste*
 ¼ *cup whipping cream*
   Pinch of cayenne pepper

1. Shell half the shrimp (about 2 cups), reserving the shells. Cover shelled shrimp and refrigerate.

2. Melt 2 tablespoons of the butter in a medium-sized, heavy saucepan over low heat. Add onion and carrot and cook, stirring often, until onion is soft but not brown (about 10 minutes). Add reserved shells and un-shelled shrimp and cook over medium heat, stirring often, until shells begin to turn pink (about 2 minutes).

3. Add wine and brandy to saucepan; bring to a boil. Add stock and a pinch of salt and white pepper; stir; bring to a boil. Reduce heat to low, cover, and simmer for 5 minutes.

4. With a slotted spoon, transfer shrimp and shells to a mortar or a large bowl. With a pestle or other heavy object, pound shrimp and shells until they are slightly crushed.

5. Return shell mixture to soup. Bring to a boil. Reduce heat to low, cover, and simmer for 10 minutes. Press soup through strainer; discard solids.

6. In a medium-sized, heavy saucepan over low heat, melt 3 tablespoons of the butter. Whisk in flour. Cook over low heat, whisking constantly, until mixture turns light beige (about 3 minutes). Remove from heat.

7. Gradually ladle soup into flour mixture, whisking. Bring to a boil over medium-high heat, whisking constantly. Reduce heat to medium-low; whisk in tomato paste, and simmer, uncovered, whisking often, 5 minutes. Add cream; bring soup to a boil, whisking.

8. Reduce heat so soup just simmers. Add shelled shrimp and cook, uncovered, over low heat, stirring occasionally, until just tender (about 2 minutes).

9. Stir in remaining tablespoon butter, heating soup just until it is absorbed. Add cayenne. Taste and add salt and white pepper, if needed. Ladle bisque into shallow bowls, distributing shrimp equally, and serve.

Serves 4.

HEARTY SOUPS

These soups, prepared all over the world, are the symbol of simple, wholesome country cooking. They can contain a variety of meats, fish, and vegetables, and make a satisfying first course or even a main dish. Hearty soups bear a certain similarity to stews, although they are not quite as thick. When made with meat, they often do not require stock because the meat flavors the soup. Hearty fish and vegetable soups, however, taste best when prepared with stock.

Most of these soups lend themselves to a variety of additions. They gain liveliness from seasonal vegetables, almost any herb, and many spices. Dried beans, potatoes, pasta, and rice are always suitable.

Although hearty soups require somewhat longer simmering than other types, a good deal of the cooking requires little attention. In addition, the long-simmered meat and vegetable soups reheat well and, like stews, taste even better the next day.

SPICY BEEF SOUP WITH GARBANZO BEANS AND RICE

This thick, country-style soup has flavors reminiscent of the cuisines of Mexico and the Near East. The soup is satisfying enough to be served as a main course followed by a green salad or other simple salad.

  ½ *cup dried garbanzo beans (chick-peas or ceci beans)*
  5 *cups water*
  1 *pound beef chuck roast*
  2 *medium onions, chopped*
  1 *teaspoon ground cumin*
     Salt and pepper
  2 *tablespoons salad oil*
  3 *tablespoons chopped cilantro*
  4 *large cloves garlic, minced*
  ¼ *pound green beans, ends removed, broken in 1-inch pieces*
  ⅓ *cup long-grain white rice*
  1 *tablespoon tomato paste*
     Pinch of cayenne pepper

1. Pick over garbanzo beans, discarding pebbles and broken or discolored beans. Rinse beans, drain, and place in a large bowl; add 3 cups water. Cover and let stand for at least 8 hours or overnight; drain, discarding soaking liquid. *Or,* to shorten the soaking, place beans in a medium saucepan with 4 cups water; bring to a boil; then boil briskly, uncovered, for 2 minutes. Remove from heat, cover, and let stand for 1 hour. Drain, discarding soaking liquid.

2. Place beans in a saucepan. Add 3 cups of the water and bring to a boil. Reduce heat to low, cover, and simmer for 30 minutes.

3. Cut beef in 1-inch cubes, trimming any large pieces of fat. Add remaining 2 cups water to saucepan of beans. Add beef cubes and bring to a boil, skimming foam. Add 1¼ cups of the chopped onions, cumin, and a pinch of salt and pepper. Reduce heat to low, cover, and simmer until beef and beans are tender (about 1 hour).

4. Heat oil in a medium frying pan over low heat. Add remaining onion and cook, stirring often, for 5 minutes. Add 2 tablespoons cilantro and cook, stirring often, until onion is tender (about 5 minutes).

5. Add sautéed onion mixture and minced garlic to soup. Add green beans and bring to a boil. Sprinkle in rice and stir. Reduce heat to medium-low and simmer, uncovered, until rice is tender (about 22 minutes).

6. Stir in tomato paste and bring to a boil. Soup can be prepared ahead up to this point and kept, covered, up to 2 days in refrigerator.

7. Reheat soup, if necessary, over medium-low heat, covered. Stir in cayenne and remaining cilantro. Taste and add more salt and pepper, if needed. Serve hot.

Serves 8 as a first course or 4 as a main course.

MINESTRONE WITH PASTA AND PESTO

This zesty Italian soup is made from a variety of colorful vegetables. In addition to or instead of some of the vegetables below, you can use green beans, pumpkin, winter squash, spinach, a small amount of turnip, and other seasonal vegetables. The most tender vegetables go into the pot last so that they retain their character. Pasta cooks directly in the soup and thickens it slightly. Any leftover soup is delicious cold.

Pesto, a special basil-and-garlic sauce, is the star of the soup. Stir it into the soup at the last minute, only after you remove the soup from the heat, to retain the pesto's fresh, zesty flavor. Although pesto is traditionally pounded in a mortar and pestle, it is much easier to prepare in a food processor. Pesto is also delicious with pasta, cooked vegetables, and fish.

½ cup dried white beans, such as Great Northern
10 cups water
¼ cup olive oil
2 medium onions, chopped
2 stalks celery, cut in thin slices
1 pound tomatoes, peeled, seeded, and chopped
½ teaspoon dried thyme
2 small carrots, peeled and diced
1 large potato, peeled and diced
4 Swiss chard leaves, cut in thin strips
2 cups Chicken Stock (see page 20)
Salt and pepper
4 small zucchini (about 1 lb total), cut in cubes
½ cup shelled fresh peas (½ lb unshelled)
1 cup medium noodles
Grated Parmesan cheese, for garnish

Pesto

3 large cloves garlic, peeled
1 bunch fresh basil (about 1 oz), leaves only (2 leaves reserved for soup)
½ cup freshly grated Parmesan cheese
2 tablespoons pine nuts
⅓ cup good-quality olive oil

1. Pick over beans, discarding pebbles and broken or discolored beans. Rinse beans, drain, and place in a large bowl; add 3 cups water. Cover and let stand for at least 8 hours or overnight; drain, discarding soaking liquid. *Or,* to shorten the soaking period, place beans in a medium saucepan with 4 cups water; bring to a boil; then boil briskly, uncovered, for 2 minutes. Remove from heat, cover, and let stand for 1 hour. Drain, discarding soaking liquid.

2. Put beans in a large saucepan with 6 cups water. Bring to a boil over medium heat and simmer, uncovered, for 1 hour, adding hot water occasionally so that beans remain covered. Drain beans, reserving ¾ cup of their liquid. Pour this reserved liquid back over beans.

3. Heat olive oil in large saucepan over low heat, add onions, and cook until soft but not brown (about 10 minutes). Add celery, tomatoes, and thyme and cook over medium heat, stirring, for 5 minutes.

4. Add carrots, potato, Swiss chard, basil leaves reserved from Pesto, beans in their reserved liquid, remaining 4 cups water, chicken stock, and a pinch of salt and pepper and bring to a boil. Reduce heat to low, cover, and simmer for 25 minutes. Add zucchini and simmer until vegetables are very tender (about 20 minutes).

5. Prepare Pesto.

6. Add peas and noodles to soup and simmer until just tender (about 10 minutes). Remove from heat, ladle into a tureen, and stir in Pesto. Taste and add more salt and pepper, if needed. Serve immediately with grated Parmesan cheese at the table.

Serves 8.

Pesto

1. Chop garlic in a food processor fitted with the metal blade by dropping cloves down feed tube one by one while blade is turning.

2. Add basil, cheese, pine nuts, and olive oil; purée. Scrape down sides of container; process until mixture is well blended. Reserve at room temperature.

LIGHT SEA BASS CHOWDER WITH TOMATOES, ZUCCHINI, AND FRESH TARRAGON

This delicate soup, which is light in both color and texture, makes an elegant first course before an entrée of roast or grilled chicken or beef. Served with French or Italian bread, it's a delightful lunch.

½ pound sea bass fillets
1 tablespoon butter
1 medium onion, chopped
2 medium-sized oval white boiling potatoes (about ½ lb total)
3 cups Fish Stock (see page 21)
Salt and pepper
2 small zucchini (about ½ lb total), quartered lengthwise and cut in ¼-inch pieces
1 cup whipping cream
1 large tomato, peeled, seeded, drained well, and diced
2 tablespoons chopped fresh tarragon leaves

1. Check fish for bones by running your fingers over it. Pull out any bones with tweezers or paring knife. Cut into 1- by 1- by ½-inch chunks.

2. Melt butter in a large saucepan. Add onion and cook over low heat, stirring, until softened (about 10 minutes).

3. Peel potatoes and halve them lengthwise. Set each half flat side down and halve them again lengthwise. Cut in thin crosswise slices about ⅛ inch thick.

4. Add potatoes, fish stock, and a pinch of salt and pepper to saucepan, stir, and bring to a boil. Reduce heat to low, cover, and simmer 7 minutes. Add zucchini and bring to a boil. Reduce heat to low and cook, uncovered, until vegetables are tender (about 4 minutes).

5. Stir ½ cup of the cream into soup and bring to a boil. Add fish, reduce heat to low, and simmer, uncovered, until fish is barely tender (about 2 minutes). Add tomato and simmer for 1 minute. Add remaining ½ cup cream and bring to a boil.

6. Remove from heat and stir in tarragon. Taste and add more salt and pepper, if needed. Serve hot.

Serves 6 as a first course or 3 as a light main course.

Light Sea Bass Chowder combines chunks of poached fish, diced vegetables, and fresh tarragon in a creamy, delicately flavored broth.

A smooth, buttery sauce is an easy and elegant way to transform asparagus—or any vegetable, fish, or light meat—into a festive dish.

Sauces

Sauces are the glory of the greatest cuisines. Surprisingly, however, the principles of sauce-making are simple. Once you've learned the basic techniques given in this chapter for white, brown, tomato, butter, and flourless cream sauces and for dressings, you can prepare endless variations. This chapter includes many of the classics, such as Madeira Sauce (page 40), Hollandaise Sauce (page 42), and Beurre Blanc (page 44), as well as a helpful chart for matching sauces with foods (see page 35).

THE PRINCIPLES OF SAUCE-MAKING

Although some people find sauces mysterious and believe that only cooks with a special talent can make a good sauce, the principles of sauce-making are simple, similar to those of soup-making. A sauce is basically a thickened liquid. The liquid usually is stock, milk, cream, melted butter, or wine, but sometimes other liquids are used. The most common thickeners are flour or other starches and egg yolks. Some sauces contain no thickener but gain their body by being reduced or boiled until they are concentrated. Once a liquid has been thickened, it needs only seasonings to give it flavor.

Sauces can be thought of as belonging to groups or families. They are categorized according to their major ingredient and their thickening agent. This chapter presents the major sauce families:

□ white and brown sauces, which are thickened with flour and made with milk or stock;

□ tomato sauces;

□ butter sauces;

□ flourless cream sauces, which are thickened by reduction;

□ dressings.

Once you know the technique for preparing the basic sauce in each family, all the rest are simple to make because they are just variations. Many sauces are easy to master; just follow the step-by-step instructions. Surprisingly, most can be prepared quickly as well.

Each family of sauces has different uses. In general, the white sauces, butter sauces, and flourless cream sauces are served with seafood, light meats, and vegetables, while the brown sauces are served with dark meats. Dressings, of course, are for salads. However, because saucing is largely a question of taste, there are many exceptions to these guidelines.

Sauces also appear in other parts of this book. Some, called compound or flavored butters, are simply softened butter mixed with flavorings. Usually served with grilled or broiled meats and fish, they are discussed on page 110.

Once you master the techniques of preparing a sauce properly, you can vary the taste of the sauce to your heart's content. If you like mustard, try adding it to Velouté Sauce (see page 38) or Brown Sauce (see pages 39 and 40). When basil is in season, use it to flavor your Hollandaise Sauce (see page 42) or Vinaigrette Dressing (see page 49). Experimenting with flavorings in sauces is one of the greatest delights of cooking. Remember, however, that sauces are meant to enhance and not to disguise the flavor of food. Add new seasonings gradually and taste the sauce before adding any additional flavor.

How to Reduce Stocks

Stocks are reduced, or boiled until concentrated, if they seem weak in flavor or if they are used for flourless cream sauces. They should be strained before they are reduced.

To reduce a stock, boil it in a wide saucepan over high heat. The larger the surface area of the pan, the faster the liquid can evaporate.

Be careful when reducing small amounts of stock (less than ½ cup) because these can burn if boiled over high heat.

Serving

There are several ways to serve sauces; the choice is up to you. You can pour a sauce over a dish, spoon a sauce onto the plate or platter and set the food on top, or serve it separately in a sauceboat or bowl. Often the decision depends on how the food looks. If you want to show off a beautiful grilled salmon steak, for example, do not cover it with sauce; either spoon a little sauce onto the plate and set the salmon on top, or serve the sauce separately. Poached chicken breasts, by contrast, look more attractive topped with a colorful sauce. If your guests are dieting, it is thoughtful to serve most or all of the sauce on the side so they can take only as much as they want.

Some sauces, such as Fresh Tomato Sauce (see page 41) or Tartar Sauce With Green Peppercorns (see page 48), are too thick to be poured over the food and should be spooned on the side.

When planning a meal, allow about ¼ cup of sauce per person.

Equipment

Little special equipment is needed for sauce-making. Use heavy saucepans of good quality so that flour-thickened sauces will not stick or burn and egg yolks will not curdle. A small whisk, which can quickly and easily reach all parts of the saucepan, is also essential.

A food processor is an invaluable aid in making some sauces, especially those in the mayonnaise family, which otherwise require prolonged whisking.

SUGGESTIONS FOR MATCHING SAUCES WITH FOODS

Sauces (pages 36–49)	Fish/Seafood (hot)	Fish/Seafood (cold)	Chicken/Turkey (hot)	Chicken/Turkey (cold)	Duck	Eggs	Beef	Veal	Lamb	Pork	Cooked Vegetables (hot)	Cooked Vegetables (cold)	Raw Vegetables	Pasta (hot)	Pasta (cold)
Cream Sauce	•					•					•			•	
Parmesan Cheese Sauce			•			•					•			•	
Creamy Velouté Sauce	•		•					•						•	
Chicken Velouté Sauce With Mushrooms			•					•						•	
Brown Sauce With Herbs			•*		•		•		•	•					
Tomato-Mushroom Sauce With Tarragon			•*			•	•	•	•	•			•		
Madeira Sauce					•		•	•							
Fresh Tomato Sauce	•		•			•	•	•	•	•	•			•	
Tomato Velouté Sauce	•		•			•		•						•	
Hollandaise Sauce	•					•					•				
Béarnaise Sauce	•					•	•		•						
Beurre Blanc	•		•								•				
Mustard Cream Sauce	•		•					•		•	•			•	
Curry Cream Sauce	•		•			•		•		•	•				
Vinaigrette Dressing	•	•		•	•		•	•			•	•	•		•
Vinaigrette With Capers	•	•					•	•		•		•	•		•
Walnut Dressing	•	•		•				•				•	•		
Garlic and Lemon Dressing	•	•		•			•					•	•		•
Pesto (see page 30)	•		•		•		•					•	•	•	•
Blue Cheese Dressing				•		•						•	•		•
Raspberry Vinegar and Shallot Dressing				•	•										
Thick Mustard Vinaigrette				•				•		•		•	•		
Mayonnaise		•		•		•						•	•		•
Spinach Sauce		•		•		•						•	•		•
Tartar Sauce With Green Peppercorns	•	•										•			
Sour Cream and Herb Dressing	•		•								•	•			

*Roast

WHITE SAUCES

White sauces are the simplest of the hot sauces. They are quickly made with ingredients usually at hand. This group can be divided further into two families: the milk-based white sauces and the stock-based, cream-colored velouté sauces.

The techniques for making both types of sauces are similar. Both are thickened with a light roux, a mixture of butter and flour that is cooked until it is bubbling. The liquid is added only after the roux cooks long enough to toast the flour lightly. If the roux is not properly cooked, or if too much flour is used for the amount of liquid, the sauce becomes unpleasantly pasty and sticky.

Flour tends to cause lumps if it is not combined properly with the liquid. The secret of making a lump-free sauce is to whisk the liquid into the roux. A whisk is much more efficient than a spoon because a whisk blends the mixture more thoroughly. If the mixture is constantly stirred with a whisk as the liquid is added and until the sauce comes to a boil, the sauce should have no lumps.

The roux gives these sauces a creamy texture, but often they are enriched with cream and egg yolks as well. With or without this addition, white sauces can be quite rich, but they are lower in calories than butter sauces or flourless cream sauces.

When they are made well, these smooth, delicate sauces are good partners for many foods. Almost all vegetables can be served with white sauces, as can light-meat chicken and turkey, fish, and shellfish. For poultry and seafood, velouté is generally preferred because the stock is "related" to the dish. Fish stock reinforces the fish flavor, and poultry stock enhances the flavor of the chicken or turkey.

Almost any flavoring can be added to these basic sauces. Cheeses are popular additions to milk-based sauces, from the mild Swiss cheeses to the sharper Parmesan or the tangy blue cheeses. Fresh herbs, Dijon mustard, and spices such as curry powder and paprika also add excitement.

White sauces can be made up to two days ahead and then refrigerated or frozen. If they are to be enriched with egg yolks, however, it is best to add these after the sauce has been reheated. Reheat white sauces in a medium saucepan over low heat, whisking often.

BASIC WHITE SAUCE

This sauce, also known as *béchamel* sauce, is the basis for a group of derivative sauces that are often served with vegetables but also accompany eggs, fish, pasta, and sometimes poultry. The basic sauce is rarely served as is. Instead it is made into other sauces, such as those given here, or is mixed with cooked vegetables to make creamed vegetables. Often the sauce is poured over vegetables, sprinkled with grated cheese, and baked as a gratin. Béchamel is sometimes layered in baked lasagne and is the secret to making macaroni and cheese creamy. A thicker version of this sauce, made with more flour, is the base for soufflés; a thinner version, made with less flour, is the foundation for cream soups.

> 1   cup milk
> 1½ tablespoons butter
> 1½ tablespoons flour
>   Salt and white pepper
>   Freshly ground or grated
>   nutmeg

1. Bring milk to a boil in a small, heavy saucepan. Remove from heat.

2. Melt butter in a small, heavy saucepan over low heat. Whisk in flour. Cook, whisking constantly, until mixture is well blended and bubbly (about 2 minutes). Remove from heat and let cool slightly.

3. Gradually pour milk into flour mixture, whisking. Return pan to heat and bring to a boil over medium-high heat, whisking constantly. Add pinch of salt, pepper, and nutmeg. Reduce heat to medium-low and simmer, uncovered, whisking often, for 5 minutes.

4. Taste and add more salt, pepper, and nutmeg, if needed. If not using sauce at once, dab top with butter to prevent a skin from forming. Sauce can be refrigerated, covered, up to 2 days, or frozen. To reheat, whisk over medium heat. Serve hot.

Makes 1 cup.

CREAM SAUCE

The quickest way to use Basic White Sauce is to turn it into Cream Sauce. Serve this delicate sauce with hard-cooked eggs, pasta, fish, or poultry. It is good with any cooked vegetable, especially spinach, broccoli, and asparagus.

> 1   cup Basic White Sauce
>   (at left)
> ¼   cup whipping cream
>   Salt and white pepper
>   Freshly ground or grated
>   nutmeg

1. Bring white sauce to a simmer in a small, heavy saucepan over medium heat, whisking often. Whisk in cream. Simmer sauce, whisking often, until slightly thickened (about 2 minutes).

2. Taste and add salt, pepper, and nutmeg, if needed. Serve hot.

Makes 1 cup.

Cream Sauce With Fresh Herbs
After removing Cream Sauce from heat, stir in 1 tablespoon chopped fresh chives, tarragon, parsley, or basil.

PARMESAN CHEESE SAUCE

Cheese sauce adds zest to vegetables, eggs, pasta, fish, and poultry. Often, the sauce is spooned over food to be baked.

Parmesan is the best cheese to use because it has an intense flavor and does not become stringy when heated. Freshly grated imported Parmesan cheese has the best flavor. Other cheeses, especially Gruyère or sharp Cheddar, may be used instead. Because all these cheeses are naturally salty, additional salt may not be needed.

If the sauce tops a dish that will be baked, add an egg yolk to help the dish brown nicely; after adding the yolk, do not reheat the sauce because it may curdle. If you are serving the sauce as an accompaniment, enrich it with butter instead of egg yolk.

1 cup Basic White Sauce
(see opposite page)
¼ cup grated Parmesan cheese
1 egg yolk or 2 tablespoons
butter
Salt and white pepper

1. Bring white sauce to a simmer in a small, heavy saucepan over medium heat, whisking often.

2. Remove from heat and whisk in cheese. Quickly whisk in egg yolk or butter (see introduction above). Taste and add salt and pepper, if needed. Serve hot.

Makes 1 cup.

A quick, easy-to-make white sauce combined with grated Parmesan cheese transforms blanched broccoli into a golden gratin.

Chicken Velouté Sauce With Mushrooms is based on Velouté Sauce made with chicken stock. Cream and an egg yolk, whisked in, give it a velvety richness and a creamy color.

VELOUTÉ SAUCE

Like Basic White Sauce (see page 36), Velouté Sauce is generally used as a base for other sauces served with fish, chicken, turkey, veal, and eggs. Often the fish, poultry, or meat is poached in stock, and this stock, which has gained more flavor, is then used to prepare the velouté.

> 1 cup Chicken Stock (see page 20) or Fish Stock (see page 21)
> 1½ tablespoons butter
> 1½ tablespoons flour
> Salt and white pepper

1. Bring stock to a boil in a small, heavy saucepan. Remove from heat.

2. Melt butter in a small, heavy saucepan over low heat. Whisk in flour. Cook, whisking constantly, until mixture turns a light beige color (about 3 minutes). Remove from heat and let cool slightly.

3. Gradually pour stock into flour mixture, whisking. Bring to a boil over medium-high heat, whisking constantly. Add pinch of salt and pepper. Reduce heat to medium-low and simmer, uncovered, whisking often, for 5 minutes.

4. Taste and add more salt and pepper, if needed. If not using sauce at once, dab top with butter to prevent a skin from forming. Sauce can be refrigerated, covered, up to 1 day or frozen.

Makes 1 cup.

Creamy Velouté Sauce Bring Velouté Sauce to a simmer in a medium-sized, heavy saucepan, whisking often. Whisk in ¼ cup whipping cream and bring to a boil. Simmer, whisking occasionally, until sauce thickens slightly (about 2 minutes). Taste and add salt and white pepper, if needed.

Creamy Velouté Sauce With Fresh Herbs After removing Creamy Velouté Sauce from heat, stir in 1 tablespoon chopped fresh chives, tarragon, parsley, basil, or dill.

TOMATO VELOUTÉ SAUCE

This orange-colored sauce combines the tanginess of tomato sauce with the smoothness of a velouté. It is perfect with fish, seafood, and chicken.

> ¼ cup Fresh Tomato Sauce (see page 41)
> 1 cup Velouté Sauce (at left)
> 2 tablespoons butter, cut in 2 pieces
> 1 tablespoon chopped parsley (optional)
> Salt and pepper

1. Purée tomato sauce in a food processor or blender until smooth.

2. Bring Velouté Sauce to a boil in a medium-sized, heavy saucepan over medium heat. Whisk in tomato sauce and bring to a simmer. Remove from heat and whisk in butter and parsley (if used) until blended. Taste and add salt and pepper, if needed. Serve hot.

Makes about 1¼ cups.

CHICKEN VELOUTÉ SAUCE WITH MUSHROOMS

Serve this sauce with poached chicken, poached or hard-cooked eggs, or roast turkey. To serve the sauce with seafood, make it with fish stock instead of chicken stock. Like other sauces containing egg yolks, it should not be reheated.

4 small mushrooms, halved and thinly sliced
3 tablespoons water
1 teaspoon butter
1 teaspoon strained fresh lemon juice
Salt and white pepper
1 cup Velouté Sauce made with chicken stock (see opposite page)
1 egg yolk
¼ cup whipping cream
1 tablespoon chopped parsley (optional)

1. Put mushrooms in a small, heavy saucepan with water, butter, lemon juice, salt, and pepper. Cover and cook over high heat until tender (about 3 minutes). Drain, reserving mushrooms and liquid separately.

2. Bring velouté to a simmer in a small, heavy saucepan over medium heat, whisking. Whisk in mushroom cooking liquid. Simmer, whisking often, until sauce is thick enough to coat a spoon. Remove from heat. Sauce can be kept, covered, up to 1 day in refrigerator.

3. Whisk egg yolk and cream in a bowl until blended. Gradually whisk about ¼ cup of sauce into egg yolk mixture. Whisk this mixture into sauce remaining in saucepan. Heat over low heat, whisking, until slightly thickened; do not boil.

4. Stir in mushrooms and parsley. Taste and add more salt and pepper, if needed. Serve hot.

Makes about 1¼ cups.

BROWN SAUCES

Like white sauces, brown sauces are thickened with a roux of butter and flour cooked together. The roux for brown sauces is cooked until it is deep brown. This dark roux will give color to the sauce. The liquid used in the sauce, usually beef or veal stock, also adds a warm brown color.

Brown sauces are served mainly with dark meats, especially beef and lamb, and with duck, although they are good with other roast poultry and poached eggs as well. They reinforce the taste of meat and enhance it with additional flavorings. Brown sauces are not served with seafood or vegetables, although vegetables can accompany the meats served with these sauces.

These sauces are often served on the side, for example, as an accompaniment to a beautifully browned roast or steak, so as not to hide the color of the food. They are not usually thick, but moisten the food without coating it or clinging to it.

A common flavoring for brown sauces is wine, especially a fortified wine such as port or Madeira. The flavor and color of tomatoes also complement these sauces. Fresh herbs are another popular addition. A small amount of butter can be stirred into the sauces, but often this enrichment is not necessary because the meat they accompany is rich enough.

Brown sauces can be made two days ahead and refrigerated or frozen. Reheat them in a heavy saucepan over medium heat, whisking often. If they contain fresh herbs or fortified wines, add more of these flavorings after reheating to compensate for flavor lost during chilling and reheating.

BASIC BROWN SAUCE

This rich, meat-flavored sauce is the basis for all brown sauces. It is generally not used as is, but is flavored with Madeira, mushrooms, or other ingredients, as in the recipes that follow. These sauces are served mainly with beef and lamb, as well as some poultry and egg dishes. Brown Sauce freezes well and can be used as needed to turn any broiled, roasted, or sautéed meat into a festive dish.

For speedy versions of Basic Brown Sauce and its variations, use Quick Brown Sauce (page 40).

2 tablespoons salad oil
2½ tablespoons flour
2 cups Beef Stock or Brown Veal Stock (see page 21)
1 onion, coarsely chopped
1 carrot, diced
1 tomato, diced
1 bay leaf
1 sprig fresh thyme or a pinch of dried thyme
5 parsley stems
2 teaspoons tomato paste
Salt and pepper

1. Heat oil in a medium-sized, heavy saucepan over low heat. Add flour and cook, whisking constantly, until mixture is golden brown. Be careful not to let it burn. Remove from heat.

2. Gradually whisk stock into flour mixture. Add onion, carrot, tomato, bay leaf, thyme, and parsley. Bring to a boil, stirring constantly. Reduce heat to low and simmer, uncovered, stirring frequently, for 1 hour.

3. Stir tomato paste into sauce, season lightly with salt and pepper, and simmer 1 minute. Strain through a fine sieve. If not using sauce at once, dab top with butter to prevent a skin from forming. Sauce can be refrigerated, covered, up to 3 days, or frozen.

Makes about 1½ cups.

QUICK BROWN SAUCE

This version of brown sauce is lighter in color and texture and its flavor is not quite as rich, but it requires less time and can be substituted for Basic Brown Sauce (page 39).

> 1 tablespoon salad oil
> 1 onion, diced
> 1 carrot, diced
> 2 cups Beef Stock (see page 21), Brown Veal Stock (see page 21), or Chicken Stock (see page 20)
> 2 ripe, medium-sized fresh tomatoes or 4 drained canned plum tomatoes, diced
> 4 tablespoons cold water
> 1 tablespoon tomato paste
> 1 tablespoon potato starch or cornstarch
> Salt and pepper

1. Heat oil in a medium-sized, heavy saucepan over medium-high heat. Add onion and carrot and sauté, stirring often, until well browned. Be careful not to let vegetables burn.

2. Add stock and tomatoes. Bring to a boil, stirring constantly. Reduce heat to very low, cover, and simmer for 30 minutes.

3. Whisk cold water into tomato paste in a small bowl. Add potato starch or cornstarch and whisk to form a smooth paste. Gradually pour into simmering sauce, whisking constantly. Bring back to a boil, whisking. Season very lightly with salt and pepper. Strain sauce, pressing on vegetables.

4. If not using sauce immediately, dab surface with a small piece of butter to prevent a skin from forming. Sauce can be refrigerated, covered, up to 3 days, or frozen.

Makes about 1½ cups.

Brown Sauce With Herbs Bring 1 cup Basic Brown Sauce (page 39) or Quick Brown Sauce to a simmer. Remove from heat and stir in 1 to 2 tablespoons chopped fresh tarragon, chives, basil, or parsley. If desired, stir in 1 tablespoon butter.

Madeira Sauce dresses up any roast poultry or meat. It can be prepared in just a few minutes if you keep brown sauce in the freezer.

MADEIRA SAUCE

Serve with grilled or sautéed steaks or with roast beef, veal, chicken, or turkey.

> 1½ cups Basic Brown Sauce (see page 39) or Quick Brown Sauce (at right)
> 4 tablespoons Madeira
> Salt and pepper
> 1 tablespoon butter (optional)

1. Bring brown sauce to a boil in a medium-sized, heavy saucepan over medium heat, whisking often.

2. Whisk in 2 tablespoons of the Madeira, add salt and pepper, and simmer, uncovered, over medium-low heat for 10 minutes.

3. Add remaining 2 tablespoons Madeira and bring just to a simmer. Remove from heat and stir in butter, if desired. Taste and add more salt and pepper, if needed. Serve hot.

Makes about 1½ cups.

TOMATO-MUSHROOM SAUCE WITH TARRAGON

Serve this sauce with all meats, chicken, turkey, and rabbit. It is also a good accompaniment to poached eggs. To save time, substitute 2 tablespoons of tomato paste for the Fresh Tomato Sauce.

¼ cup cold butter
2 shallots, finely chopped
¼ pound mushrooms, halved and thinly sliced
½ cup dry white wine
1 cup Fresh Tomato Sauce (at right)
1 cup Basic Brown Sauce (page 39) or Quick Brown Sauce (opposite page)
Pinch of sugar (optional)
1 tablespoon chopped parsley
1 tablespoon chopped fresh tarragon or 1 teaspoon dried tarragon (optional)
Salt and pepper

1. Melt 2 tablespoons of the butter in a large frying pan over low heat. Refrigerate remaining butter. Add shallots to frying pan and cook until softened (about 2 minutes). Add mushrooms and cook over medium-high heat, tossing often, until lightly browned and tender.

2. Add wine to pan of mushrooms and boil, stirring, until liquid is reduced to about ⅓ cup. Transfer mixture to a medium-sized, heavy saucepan.

3. Add tomato sauce and brown sauce and bring to a boil, stirring. Stir in a pinch of sugar, if desired. Sauce can be prepared ahead up to this point and kept, covered, up to 2 days in refrigerator, or it can be frozen. If making it ahead, dab surface of sauce with a small piece of butter.

4. Just before serving, bring sauce to a boil. Cut remaining butter in 4 pieces. Remove sauce from heat and stir in butter, a piece at a time. Add parsley and tarragon. Taste and add salt and pepper, if needed.

Makes about 2 cups.

TOMATO SAUCES

Tomato sauces, found in many cuisines, are good with almost every food, from meats to fish and pasta.

The best tomato sauces are those made with fresh tomatoes, although canned ones can be used as well. Because tomatoes are the star ingredient and determine the final flavor of the sauce, they must be ripe. Sometimes tomatoes are misleading because they appear red on the outside but turn out to have disappointingly pale flesh. To avoid these, choose tomatoes that are not too firm and that have a strong smell of tomatoes. No extra thickening is required for most tomato sauces because the tomato pulp thickens the sauce as it cooks.

Herbs and tomatoes are natural partners. Besides the familiar tomato-loving herbs—basil, thyme, and oregano—almost any fresh herb or good-quality dried herb can flavor a tomato sauce. Members of the onion family, especially yellow onions, leeks, shallots, and garlic, can be chopped, sautéed, and cooked with the tomatoes to give added depth of flavor.

Although tomato sauce is delicious alone, it is so versatile that it can be mixed with most other sauces. Mix a few tablespoons into Basic White Sauce (see page 36) or Velouté Sauce (see page 38) to make an orange-colored sauce that is good with fish. You can combine tomato sauce with a brown sauce; Tomato-Mushroom Sauce with Tarragon (at left) is an example. Even the butter sauces, such as Béarnaise Sauce (see page 44), benefit from the tangy addition of a few spoonfuls of tomato sauce. Fresh tomato sauce mixed into Mayonnaise (see page 46) makes a delicious dressing for a variety of salads.

FRESH TOMATO SAUCE

The flavor of this chunky sauce is fresh because the tomatoes cook only briefly. The sauce is good with pasta, fish, chicken, meat, eggs, and vegetables.

There are many ways to vary the flavor of the sauce. Butter or olive oil can replace the salad oil. In addition to thyme and bay leaf, a variety of fresh herbs can be added to the finished sauce; basil is especially good, but tarragon, oregano, and cilantro (fresh coriander) also add an interesting change of flavor. If the color of the sauce is not bright enough, mix in a tablespoon of tomato paste.

When tomatoes are out of season, the sauce can be made with 2½ pounds (undrained weight) of canned whole plum tomatoes; drain them well and chop them.

2 tablespoons salad oil
Half an onion, chopped
1 clove garlic, finely chopped
2½ pounds ripe tomatoes, peeled, seeded, and chopped (see page 13)
Pinch of dried thyme
1 bay leaf
Salt and pepper

1. Heat oil in a medium-sized, heavy frying pan over low heat. Add onion and cook, stirring occasionally, until soft but not browned (about 7 minutes). Stir in garlic and cook 30 seconds.

2. Add tomatoes, thyme, bay leaf, salt, and pepper. Cook over medium heat, stirring often, until tomatoes are soft and mixture is thick and smooth (about 20 minutes).

3. Discard bay leaf. Taste and add more salt and pepper, if needed. Sauce can be refrigerated, covered, up to 2 days, or frozen. Serve hot.

Makes about 1½ cups.

Smooth Tomato Sauce For a very smooth sauce, purée Fresh Tomato Sauce in a food processor or blender.

...ON SAUCES

White and Brown Sauces

☐ *Be sure the saucepan is dry before making a roux.*

☐ *Always whisk all over the surface of the pan, including the edges, to avoid sticking.*

☐ *When making a white or brown sauce ahead, dab the surface of the hot sauce with soft butter to prevent a skin from forming.*

☐ *Thaw frozen white and brown sauces before reheating.*

Butter Sauces

☐ *Add the butter gradually to hollandaise and béarnaise sauces; otherwise they may separate.*

☐ *If a hollandaise or béarnaise sauce separates, whisk 1 tablespoon of the separated sauce with 1 tablespoon of cold water until the mixture is smooth. Gradually whisk in the remaining separated sauce. If this does not work, start again by whisking 1 egg yolk and 1 tablespoon of water in a small, heavy saucepan over low heat until thick, as in the recipes; then very gradually whisk in the separated sauce and any remaining clarified butter.*

Dressings

☐ *All vinaigrettes can be made ahead but will separate upon standing. To re-emulsify them, simply shake or whisk them.*

☐ *When making mayonnaise, add the oil to the yolks slowly; otherwise, the mayonnaise separates.*

☐ *If mayonnaise separates, beat it gradually into 1 teaspoon of Dijon mustard or 1 egg yolk.*

BUTTER SAUCES

This is probably the most popular group of sauces. They are rich and silky in texture because their main ingredient, butter, is not only an enrichment but also constitutes the body of the sauce. These sauces are reserved for special occasions and for the most festive foods, such as lobster, scallops, fresh salmon, and asparagus.

Although these sauces can be made quickly, they also demand the most care. They can separate if they are not prepared carefully. They are emulsions, or fragile combinations of fat (in this case heated butter) and liquid. If the butter separates from the liquid, the sauce loses its lovely texture and becomes watery and unattractive. Hollandaise and béarnaise sauces, which contain egg yolks in addition to the butter, lose their smoothness if the egg yolks curdle, or cook into small bits resembling scrambled eggs. To avoid both problems, whisk the sauces constantly and do not cook them too long or over too high a flame. They should be served warm, not boiling hot.

Because these sauces are so sensitive to heat, it is best not to serve them on heated plates. Often they are served separately, in sauceboats. Only a small amount of these rich sauces is needed—3 tablespoons per person is usually enough.

Butter sauces should not be prepared ahead. If some sauce is left, however, do not discard it, but store it in the refrigerator or freezer. Leftover sauce cannot be reheated to its former smoothness, but it can be whisked in small pieces into another sauce, especially a velouté or tomato sauce. Stir in small pieces of leftover butter sauces to impart a special flavor to hot cooked rice, pasta, or vegetables.

HOLLANDAISE SAUCE

Hollandaise sauce, one of the most delicate of sauces, is particularly good with poached fish, shellfish, and vegetables. It is also a delicious complement to poached eggs in dishes such as eggs Benedict. The predominant flavor in the sauce is butter. A small amount of lemon juice is added as a seasoning. Many cooks increase the amount of lemon juice, especially when they serve the sauce with fish.

Egg yolks, the thickener in hollandaise, always demand care. If the egg yolks are heated too long, they scramble. If the butter is added too quickly, the sauce separates. (To save a separated sauce, see "Tips on Sauces," at left.)

¾ cup unsalted butter
3 egg yolks
3 tablespoons water
　Salt
　Pinch of cayenne pepper
¼ teaspoon strained fresh lemon juice, or to taste

1. To clarify butter, melt it in a small, heavy saucepan over low heat. Remove from heat and skim white foam from surface. Pour remaining clear butter into a bowl, discarding white sediment in saucepan. Let clarified butter cool to lukewarm.

2. Combine egg yolks, water, and salt in a small, heavy, non-aluminum saucepan and whisk briefly. Cook over low heat, whisking vigorously and constantly, until mixture is creamy and thick enough so that whisk leaves a visible trail on bottom of pan. Be careful not to let mixture become too hot or egg yolks will curdle. Remove pan from heat occasionally so that it does not become too hot; sides of pan should be cool enough to touch. When yolk mixture becomes thick enough, remove it immediately from heat and continue to whisk for about 30 seconds.

3. With saucepan off heat, gradually whisk in clarified butter drop by drop. After sauce has absorbed about 2 or 3 tablespoons butter, add remaining butter in a very thin stream, whisking vigorously and constantly. Stir in cayenne and lemon juice. Taste and add more salt, cayenne, and lemon juice, if needed.

4. Serve sauce as soon as possible. It can be kept warm for about 15 minutes in its saucepan set on a rack above warm water, but it must be whisked frequently. It can also be kept warm in a thermos.

Makes about 1 cup.

QUICK HOLLANDAISE SAUCE

This version, prepared in a food processor or blender, can be served with the same foods as the traditional hollandaise sauce, but it is not as thick or delicate. There is no need to heat the egg yolks in a saucepan; the butter is heated until bubbling, so that it cooks the egg yolks slightly.

> ¾ cup unsalted butter
> 3 egg yolks, at room temperature
> 1 tablespoon water
> Salt
> Pinch of cayenne pepper
> ½ teaspoon strained fresh lemon juice, or to taste

1. To clarify butter, heat it in a small, heavy saucepan over low heat until it begins to bubble. Remove from heat and skim white foam from surface.

2. In a blender or food processor, process egg yolks with water and salt until they are lightened in color and very well blended. Reheat butter to just bubbling. With machine running, gradually incorporate hot butter drop by drop into yolks. After 2 or 3 tablespoons butter have been added, pour remaining butter through in a fine stream, with machine still running.

3. Add cayenne and lemon juice and process briefly to mix. Taste and add more salt, cayenne, and lemon juice, if needed.

4. Serve sauce as soon as possible. To keep it warm for about 15 minutes, transfer to a saucepan placed in a pan of warm water, but whisk it frequently. It can also be kept warm in a thermos.

Makes about 1 cup.

Quick Béarnaise Sauce Prepare the liquid flavoring for Béarnaise Sauce, page 44, step 2, and substitute it for the water in the recipe above. In step 3 above, omit lemon juice. Stir 1 tablespoon chopped tarragon and 1 tablespoon chopped parsley into finished sauce.

Hollandaise Sauce is a classic accompaniment for a number of dishes, such as poached eggs and asparagus (see page 63). Serve the dish for brunch or lunch or as a first course at dinner.

BÉARNAISE SAUCE

Béarnaise sauce is a zesty variation of hollandaise. It is prepared like a hollandaise, except that the egg yolk mixture is flavored with tarragon, vinegar, wine, and shallots. Pepper is added in two forms—as cracked peppercorns that cook in the vinegar and as freshly ground pepper at the end. Serve the sauce with broiled fish, especially salmon, with steak, or with poached eggs. (For hints on saving a separated sauce, see page 42.)

- ¾ *cup unsalted butter*
- ½ *teaspoon black peppercorns*
- 2 *tablespoons white wine vinegar*
- 3 *tablespoons dry white wine*
- 2 *shallots, chopped*
- 3 *stems fresh tarragon (without leaves), chopped*
- 3 *egg yolks*
  Salt and pepper
- 1 *tablespoon chopped fresh tarragon leaves*
- 1 *tablespoon chopped parsley*

1. Clarify butter (see step 1 of Hollandaise Sauce, page 42).

2. Crack peppercorns coarsely by pounding them a few times in a small mortar with pestle or by crushing them with a rolling pin or a heavy saucepan. Combine vinegar, wine, peppercorns, shallots, and tarragon stems in a small, heavy, non-aluminum saucepan. Simmer over medium heat until only about 2 tablespoons liquid remain. Strain, pushing hard on shallots. Return strained liquid to saucepan and let cool for 2 minutes.

3. Whisk egg yolks and a pinch of salt into liquid. Cook over low heat, whisking vigorously and constantly, until mixture is creamy and thick enough so that the whisk leaves a visible trail on bottom of pan. Be careful not to let mixture become too hot or egg yolks will curdle. Remove pan occasionally from heat so that it does not become too hot; the sides of pan should be cool enough to touch. When yolk mixture becomes thick enough, remove it immediately from heat. Continue to whisk for about 30 seconds.

4. With saucepan off heat, gradually whisk in clarified butter drop by drop. After sauce has absorbed about 2 or 3 tablespoons butter, add remaining butter in a very thin stream, whisking vigorously and constantly.

5. Add a pinch of pepper, chopped tarragon, and parsley. Taste and add salt and pepper, if needed.

6. Serve sauce as soon as possible. It can be kept warm for about 15 minutes in its pan set on a rack above warm water, but it must be whisked frequently. It can also be kept warm in a thermos.

Makes about 1 cup.

BEURRE BLANC
White butter sauce

This is the most popular butter sauce in modern French cooking and has become a great American favorite as well. It is a delicate sauce, thickened only with butter. Serve it with poached or steamed fish, shellfish, and vegetables. It is also good with poached chicken breasts. Leftover beurre blanc cannot be reheated because it would separate, but it can be used to enrich flour-thickened sauces or stirred into hot cooked vegetables, pasta, or rice instead of plain butter.

- 1 *cup cold butter, cut into 16 cubes*
- 2 *large shallots, finely chopped*
- 2 *tablespoons white wine vinegar*
- 3 *tablespoons dry white wine*
- 2 *tablespoons whipping cream*
  Salt and white pepper

1. Refrigerate butter cubes until ready to use.

2. Combine shallots, vinegar, and wine in a small, heavy, non-aluminum saucepan. Bring to a boil. Reduce heat to medium and simmer mixture, uncovered, until liquid is reduced to about 2 tablespoons.

3. Whisk in cream and reduce heat to low. Simmer mixture, whisking occasionally, until liquid is reduced to about 3 tablespoons. Mixture can be prepared up to 1 day ahead, covered, and refrigerated.

4. Reheat shallot mixture to simmer and season lightly with salt and pepper. Reduce heat to low. Add one cube of butter, whisking constantly. When butter cube is nearly blended into liquid, add another cube, still whisking. Continue adding butter cubes one at a time, whisking constantly. The sauce should be pleasantly warm to the touch and should thicken. If it becomes too hot and drops of melted butter appear, remove saucepan immediately from heat and whisk sauce well; add next 3 or 4 butter cubes off heat, whisking constantly. When temperature of sauce drops again to warm, return to low heat and continue adding remaining butter cubes. Remove from heat as soon as last butter cube is added.

5. Strain sauce if desired. Taste, and add salt and white pepper if needed.

6. Serve sauce as soon as possible. It can be kept warm for about 15 minutes in its saucepan set on a rack above a pan of warm water, but it must be whisked frequently to prevent separation. It can also be kept warm in a thermos.

Makes about 1 cup.

FLOURLESS CREAM SAUCES

The traditional cream sauce gets its body from flour. This new type of sauce is richer than the traditional ones because reduced cream gives the sauce its body; a liquid is boiled with cream until a portion of the water evaporates and the sauce thickens naturally.

These sauces are not as thick as the white sauces; they are light in texture, and are very quick to make. Nearly as rich as butter sauces, they usually contain white wine and can also be flavored with stock or with the same ingredients as any white or velouté sauce. Like white, velouté, and butter sauces, flourless cream sauces are good accompaniments to seafood, light meats, and vegetables.

The sauces in this group can be made ahead and refrigerated for up to two days. Reheat them in a heavy, uncovered saucepan, whisking often.

MUSTARD CREAM SAUCE

Serve this sauce with broiled or sautéed fish fillets, sautéed veal escalopes, chicken breasts, turkey breast slices, or pork chops. Use chicken or veal stock in a sauce to accompany poultry or meats and fish stock in a sauce for fish.

1 tablespoon butter
2 shallots, finely chopped
¼ cup dry white wine
½ cup Chicken Stock (see page 20), Brown Veal Stock (see page 21), or Fish Stock (see page 21)
Salt and pepper
1¼ cups whipping cream
1½ to 2 tablespoons Dijon mustard

1. Melt butter in a medium-sized, heavy saucepan over low heat. Add shallots and cook, stirring, until softened (about 2 minutes).

2. Add wine, stock, salt, and pepper and simmer, stirring, until liquid is reduced to about 2 tablespoons. Stir in cream and bring to a boil, stirring. Reduce heat to medium and cook, stirring often, until sauce is thick enough to coat a spoon (about 7 minutes). Sauce can be kept, covered, up to 1 day in refrigerator.

3. Reheat sauce, if necessary, in medium-sized saucepan over medium heat, whisking. Reduce heat to low and whisk in 1½ tablespoons mustard. Taste and add more salt, pepper, and mustard, if needed. Serve hot.

Makes about 1 cup.

CURRY CREAM SAUCE

This is not a hot, fiery sauce, but rather a moderately spicy sauce in which the curry powder balances the richness of the cream. Serve it with fish, shellfish, chicken, turkey, pork, cooked vegetables, or poached or hard-cooked eggs.

1 tablespoon butter
2 tablespoons finely chopped onion
1½ teaspoons curry powder
3 tablespoons dry white wine
1 tablespoon white wine vinegar
3 tablespoons water
1 cup whipping cream
Salt and pepper

1. Melt butter in a medium-sized, heavy saucepan over low heat. Add onion and cook, stirring, until soft but not browned (about 7 minutes). Add curry powder and cook, stirring, 30 seconds.

2. Add wine, vinegar, and water and simmer over medium heat until liquid is reduced to about 2 tablespoons.

3. Stir in cream, salt, and pepper, and bring to a boil, stirring. Reduce heat to medium and cook, stirring often, until sauce is thick enough to coat a spoon (about 4 minutes). Taste and add more salt and pepper, if needed. Sauce can be refrigerated, covered, up to 1 day.

Makes about ¾ cup.

DRESSINGS

Dressings (sauces used on salads) are served cold or at room temperature. The foods they accompany are also usually cold or at room temperature, although some dressings are also good with hot food. Dressings are very quick to prepare and rarely require cooking, which makes them popular for summer. Homemade dressings taste much fresher and better than commercial types and are free of preservatives.

The two basic dressings are vinaigrette and mayonnaise. Most other dressings are variations of these two. Vinaigrette is light and clear, making it ideal for greens and colorful salads, which are most appealing when the ingredients show through the dressing. It is also good with salads containing rich ingredients, such as beef or duck. Mayonnaise-based dressings are richer and creamier and complement lean ingredients, such as fish, chicken, and turkey.

Like butter sauces, dressings are emulsified sauces, or blends of fat and liquid; unlike butter sauces, dressings are not blended over heat. The ingredients are simply whisked gradually together or are whirled in a blender or food processor. Vinaigrette is not stable and therefore must be whisked just before using. An egg yolk binds mayonnaise together, making it relatively stable.

Differing versions of both types of dressings can be produced by varying the kind of vinegar and oil used, and both benefit greatly from the addition of chopped fresh herbs and condiments such as mustard, capers, and chopped olives.

MAYONNAISE

Use mayonnaise with any type of salad except green salads. The basic recipe can be varied in many ways. Use a neutral vegetable oil, or replace part of it with olive oil or other oils to give a special flavor. Almost any fresh herb can be added.

Mayonnaise can be made in a bowl, a blender, or a food processor. If you use a large food processor, do not try to halve the recipe; the processor will not adequately blend the ingredients.

When you prepare the mayonnaise in a blender or food processor, you can use one whole large egg instead of two yolks, if you wish. In this case, reduce the oil quantity to 1¼ cups. This mayonnaise will not be quite as rich or as thick as one made with egg yolks alone. (For hints on what to do if mayonnaise separates, see "Tips on Sauces" on page 42.)

Mayonnaise can be refrigerated, covered, up to 1 week.

> 2 egg yolks, at room
>   temperature
>   Salt and white pepper
> 1 teaspoon Dijon mustard
> 2 tablespoons white wine
>   vinegar or strained fresh
>   lemon juice
> 1½ cups salad oil at room
>   temperature
> 1 tablespoon warm water
>   (optional)

To prepare with a whisk or a mixer:

1. Whisk egg yolks with a pinch of salt, pepper, mustard, and 1 tablespoon of the vinegar in a medium-sized, heavy bowl.

2. Begin whisking or beating in oil drop by drop. When 2 or 3 tablespoons oil have been added, whisk or beat in remaining oil in a very fine stream. Stir in remaining vinegar. Taste and add more salt and pepper, if needed.

3. If mayonnaise is too thick, gradually beat in 1 tablespoon warm water.

Makes about 1½ cups.

To prepare with a food processor or blender:

1. Process yolks with a pinch of salt, pepper, mustard, 1 tablespoon of the vinegar, and 1 tablespoon of the oil in a blender or food processor until well blended.

2. With machine running, pour in remaining oil, about 1 teaspoon at a time. After ¼ cup oil has been added, pour in remaining oil in a fine stream, with machine still running. Add remaining tablespoon vinegar and process briefly to blend. Taste and add more salt and pepper, if needed.

3. If mayonnaise is too thick, gradually beat in 1 tablespoon warm water.

Makes about 1½ cups.

SOUR CREAM AND HERB DRESSING

Sour cream gives mayonnaise a lighter texture and a delicate flavor. This dressing is good with almost any food served cold: cooked fish, shellfish, chicken, turkey, cooked vegetables. It also makes a good dip for raw vegetables. Other fresh herbs, such as basil or cilantro, can be substituted for the tarragon and chives.

> ½ cup sour cream
> ¾ cup Mayonnaise (at left)
> 1 tablespoon chopped parsley
> 1 tablespoon thinly sliced chives
> 1 tablespoon chopped fresh
>   tarragon leaves
> 1 teaspoon strained fresh lemon
>   juice (optional)
>   Salt and pepper

1. Mix sour cream with mayonnaise in a medium-sized bowl until smooth. Stir in parsley, chives, and tarragon.

2. Taste and add lemon juice (if used) and salt and pepper, if needed. Dressing can be refrigerated, covered, up to 2 days.

Makes about 1¼ cups.

SPINACH SAUCE

This delicate green sauce is prepared quickly in the food processor. Serve it with cold poached fish, seafood, chicken breasts, turkey, or hard-cooked eggs or as a dipping sauce for vegetables. The sauce also makes a good dressing for pasta salads.

To prepare the sauce without a food processor, chop the cooked spinach and herbs as finely as possible with a heavy knife and whirl them with the mayonnaise in a blender or whisk them into the mayonnaise in a bowl. When whisked by hand, the sauce will not be as smooth as one made in the food processor, but it will still be delicious.

Remember to squeeze the liquid thoroughly from the cooked greens; too much liquid can cause the sauce to separate.

> 20 spinach leaves, washed and
>   stems removed
> ⅓ cup watercress leaves
> ¼ cup small parsley sprigs
> 1 cup Mayonnaise (at left)
>   Salt and pepper
> 2 to 3 tablespoons warm water
>   (optional)

1. Plunge spinach and watercress into a medium saucepan of boiling water. Return water to a boil. Immediately pour into a colander, draining off all water. Rinse leaves in cold running water and drain thoroughly. Squeeze to remove excess liquid.

2. Purée spinach, watercress, and parsley in a food processor until smooth. If necessary, add 2 or 3 tablespoons of the mayonnaise to help make a smoother mixture.

3. Add remaining mayonnaise and process until smooth. Taste and add salt and pepper, if needed. If sauce is very thick, beat in warm water, 1 tablespoon at a time, until sauce is just thin enough to pour. Sauce can be refrigerated, covered, up to 2 days.

Makes about 1 cup.

A traditional partner for poached fish such as salmon, Spinach Sauce can be made quickly and easily in a food processor.

TARTAR SAUCE WITH GREEN PEPPERCORNS

Green peppercorns give extra zip to tartar sauce, a traditional accompaniment for fried fish. The sauce is also delicious with fried vegetables, especially cauliflower, and with cold chicken or turkey. For added interest, use green peppercorn mustard or herb mustard instead of Dijon mustard.

> 1 cup Mayonnaise (see
>   page 46)
> 1 tablespoon Dijon mustard
> 2 tablespoons chopped parsley
> 1 tablespoon chopped green
>   onion, preferably green part
> 1 hard-cooked egg, chopped
> 1 tablespoon drained capers,
>   rinsed and chopped
> 2 teaspoons drained green
>   peppercorns
> 1 tablespoon chopped dill pickle
> 1 teaspoon strained fresh lemon
>   juice (optional)
>   Salt and pepper

1. Mix mayonnaise and mustard in a bowl until thoroughly blended. Stir in parsley, green onion, egg, capers, peppercorns, and pickle.

2. Taste and add lemon juice, if desired, and salt and pepper, if needed. Sauce can be refrigerated, covered, up to 2 days.

Makes about 1¼ cups.

THICK MUSTARD VINAIGRETTE

This dressing is good with strong-flavored greens such as escarole and Belgian endive and with cold meats, especially beef, pork, and turkey. The dressing is thicker than most vinai-grettes because the oil is whisked in gradually. In addition, the mustard helps to thicken it. Instead of plain Dijon mustard, you can use a grainy mustard or a flavored Dijon mustard, such as herb mustard or green peppercorn mustard.

> 2 teaspoons Dijon mustard
> 2 tablespoons red wine vinegar
>   Salt and pepper to taste
> 6 tablespoons salad oil

1. Whisk mustard, vinegar, salt, and pepper in a small bowl. Gradually pour in oil in a fine stream, whisking constantly.

2. Taste and add more salt and pepper, if needed. Dressing can be refrigerated, covered, up to 1 week. Whisk before using.

Makes about ½ cup.

GARLIC AND LEMON DRESSING

Use this dressing to give a Mediterranean character to salads of vegetables such as green beans, sliced raw mushrooms, tomatoes, and raw or grilled green and red bell peppers. It is also good with beef, chicken, or seafood salads.

Chopped garlic gives this dressing quite a punch. For a more subtle garlic flavor, add the garlic clove whole to the dressing and refrigerate for one day before serving; remove the garlic before serving.

> 2 tablespoons strained fresh
>   lemon juice
> 1 small clove garlic, very finely
>   chopped
>   Salt and pepper to taste
> 6 tablespoons olive oil
> 1 tablespoon chopped parsley

1. Blend lemon juice, garlic, salt, and pepper in a small bowl until salt dissolves.

2. Whisk in oil. Taste and add more salt and pepper, if needed. Dressing can be stored in refrigerator, covered, up to 1 week.

3. Whisk dressing before using and add chopped parsley.

Makes ½ cup.

BLUE CHEESE DRESSING

This creamy dressing has a vinaigrette base and is enriched with whipping cream and sour cream and flavored with blue cheese. Serve it with cold chicken, turkey, or hard-cooked eggs. It adds excitement to a variety of salads, especially those containing raw or cooked vegetables and those combining chicken or turkey with greens. Be careful not to add too much salt to the dressing because blue cheese is salty.

> 1 tablespoon white wine vinegar
>   Pepper
> 3 tablespoons salad oil
> 3 tablespoons whipping cream
> 5 tablespoons sour cream
> 2 tablespoons crumbled blue
>   cheese
>   Salt (optional)

1. Combine vinegar and pepper in a bowl and whisk briefly. Gradually whisk in oil.

2. Add whipping cream gradually, whisking until mixture is well blended. Gradually whisk in sour cream. Whisk in blue cheese; small pieces will remain. Taste and add salt and more pepper, if needed.

3. Chill before using until flavors blend and dressing thickens slightly, about 30 minutes. Dressing can be refrigerated, covered, up to 2 days.

Makes about ¾ cup.

VINAIGRETTE DRESSING

This popular salad dressing is perfect for green salad because it coats the greens lightly. It is also good with almost any salad ingredient, from raw or cooked vegetables to meats, fish, and pasta. Although vinaigrette is usually associated with cold dishes, it also makes a quick and pleasant sauce for hot food, especially fish, poultry, and meat. Herb vinaigrette is especially good with seafood salads.

There are many ways to vary the basic dressing. Replace the salad oil with olive, walnut, or other oil. Use white wine vinegar or red wine vinegar for everyday dressings; or try Champagne vinegar, sherry vinegar, or tarragon vinegar for special occasions.

> 2 tablespoons wine vinegar or strained fresh lemon juice
> Salt and pepper to taste
> 6 tablespoons salad oil

1. Whisk vinegar, salt, and pepper in a small bowl until salt dissolves.

2. Whisk in oil. Taste, and add more salt and pepper, if needed. Dressing can be refrigerated, covered, up to 1 week. Whisk before using.

Makes about ½ cup.

Herb Vinaigrette Just before using, add 1 tablespoon chopped parsley, chives, basil, or tarragon. For a more intense tarragon flavor, make the dressing with tarragon vinegar and add chopped fresh tarragon.

VINAIGRETTE WITH CAPERS

This colorful dressing, dotted with green and white, is a good accompaniment to grilled fish, either hot or at room temperature, and is delicious on fish salads. Be careful with the salt because capers are salty.

> 2 tablespoons white wine vinegar
> Salt and pepper to taste
> 6 tablespoons olive oil
> 1 tablespoon drained capers, rinsed and chopped
> 2 tablespoons chopped parsley
> 1 hard-cooked egg, chopped

1. Whisk vinegar, a small pinch of salt, and pepper in a small bowl until salt dissolves. Whisk in oil, capers, and parsley. Dressing can be refrigerated, covered, up to 2 days. Whisk before continuing.

2. Stir in chopped egg. Taste and add more salt and pepper if needed.

Makes about ⅔ cup.

WALNUT DRESSING

Use this dressing for simple green salads and for salads of seafood, chicken, or turkey. If you would like a stronger walnut flavor, use only walnut oil. After opening a container of walnut oil, keep it in the refrigerator so the oil will not become rancid.

> 2 tablespoons white wine vinegar
> Salt and pepper to taste
> ¼ cup walnut oil
> 2 tablespoons salad oil
> 2 tablespoons finely chopped walnuts

1. Whisk vinegar, salt, and pepper in a small bowl until salt dissolves. Whisk in walnut oil and salad oil, then walnuts.

2. Taste and add more salt and pepper, if needed. Let stand 30 minutes so that flavors blend. Dressing can be kept, covered, up to 4 days in refrigerator. Whisk before using.

Makes about ½ cup.

RASPBERRY VINEGAR AND SHALLOT DRESSING

This pink dressing has a wonderful aroma of raspberries. Use it to flavor poultry salads and to add unexpected zip to simple green salads. The dressing is made quickly in a food processor, but it can be prepared in a blender or bowl instead if the shallot is finely chopped by hand. If you are using a blender, combine the chopped shallot with the other ingredients in step 1 and continue with the rest of the recipe. If you prefer to prepare the dressing in a bowl with a whisk, follow the procedure for Vinaigrette Dressing (at left), adding the chopped shallot at the beginning.

> Half a small shallot, peeled and halved
> 3 tablespoons raspberry vinegar
> Salt and pepper to taste
> ½ cup plus 1 tablespoon salad oil

1. Chop shallot until fine in a food processor by dropping pieces down feed tube one by one while blade is turning. Add vinegar, salt, and pepper and process until combined.

2. As blade is turning, gradually pour in oil. Dressing will thicken slightly. Taste and add more salt and pepper, if needed. Dressing can be refrigerated, covered, up to 2 days. Whisk before using.

Makes about ¾ cup.

Steaming is a particularly good method for cooking vegetables such as artichokes because it locks in both flavors and nutrients.

Steaming, Poaching & Boiling

Cooking with moist heat is the most versatile culinary technique; from steamed fish and poached chicken breasts to boiled eggs, vegetables, and pasta, it is the method used most often and for the broadest array of foods. Steamed, poached, and boiled foods stay moist and flavorful, and, since no fat is required, they are low in calories as well. With the recipes in this chapter, you can make a wide variety of superb dishes while you master the secrets of successful cooking with moist heat.

COOKING WITH MOIST HEAT

Steaming, poaching, and boiling are ways of cooking with moist heat. During poaching and boiling, foods are immersed in hot liquid, which cooks them directly. During steaming, foods cook over boiling water. A wide range of foods—fish, meat, poultry, eggs, vegetables, and even fruit—can be cooked by these techniques.

There are many reasons to cook with moist heat: It can seal in delicate flavors, draw out undesirable ones, or add new ones. Steaming and poaching are especially useful for preparing fish, shellfish, and chicken that are to be served cold or in salads; the food remains moist even after chilling. It is often convenient to poach or steam more fish or meat than needed for one meal and to save part of it for serving cold the next day. Poached meats, but not fish, can be reheated.

Cooking by these methods does not require adding fat to the food. These are, therefore, favored techniques for cooking low-calorie meals. For festive meals, however, steamed or poached foods are usually enlivened with a sauce. In fact, these are the best methods for cooking seafood that will be served with a rich sauce. Perfectly poached sole fillets or steamed scallops accompanied with a luscious Hollandaise Sauce (see page 42) show off both sauce and seafood to best advantage.

When there is no time to prepare a sauce, steamed or poached fish or shellfish are often served with melted butter for dipping.

It is important to drain poached, steamed, or boiled foods well so they will not be watery. Draining is particularly crucial if the food will be served with a sauce because excess liquid dilutes the sauce.

STEAMING

Steaming is cooking by the heat of steam. The food is placed on a rack above, but not in direct contact with, boiling liquid. The pan is covered to keep in the steam. This technique is ideal for cooking seafood because steaming preserves its delicate flavor and gives it a wonderfully moist texture. Steaming is suitable for whole fish, fillets, and fish steaks. Scallops and shrimp also are very tender and succulent when steamed.

For steaming mussels and clams, a special technique, which is actually a combination of poaching and steaming, is used. Instead of being placed in a steamer, the mollusks are placed in a saucepan with a small amount of liquid. When they are covered and heated, the steam created by the liquid forces them to open.

Vegetables, too, can be steamed. Because steaming locks in flavors, it is better for mild-tasting than strong-flavored vegetables. In addition, steaming requires more time than boiling. This method is favored by nutritionists because it preserves more of the nutrients of food than boiling and poaching do.

Several types of steamers are available. Chinese bamboo or metal steamers are convenient because the trays can be stacked and several foods can be steamed at once. You can make any deep saucepan into a steamer by setting a French folding steamer rack inside and covering the pan tightly. To steam small amounts of food, you can improvise a steamer by setting a colander or strainer in a large saucepan and covering it tightly.

STEAMED SEA BASS WITH GINGER, CARROTS, AND GREEN ONIONS

In this recipe, a whole fish is steamed on a heatproof plate instead of directly on the steamer so that the skin of the fish will not stick to the steamer tray. Steamed with a small amount of sauce, the fish is served on the steaming plate, which should be deep so that the sauce will not run off.

> 1 *whole sea bass (1½ lbs)*
>   *Salt and pepper*
> 2 *tablespoons dry sherry*
> 1 *small carrot, cut in thin strips, about 1½ by ⅛ by ⅛ inches*
> 1 *tablespoon plus 1½ teaspoons each soy sauce and water*
> ½ *teaspoon sugar*
> 1 *tablespoon salad oil*
> 1 *tablespoon minced, peeled fresh ginger root*
> 1 *tablespoon minced green onion*
> 2 *medium cloves garlic, minced*
> 2 *tablespoons very thin strips of green onion, about 1½ inches long*

1. Leave head and tail on fish. With sturdy scissors, snip fins and trim tail straight. Rinse fish inside and out, removing any scales, and pat dry.

2. Bring at least 1 inch of water to a boil in base of steamer. Boiling water should not reach holes in top part of steamer.

3. Make 3 diagonal slashes on each side of fish. Rub fish inside and out with salt, pepper, and 1 teaspoon of the sherry. Set fish on a deep heatproof plate; be sure plate fits easily in steamer top.

4. Put carrot in medium saucepan, cover with water, and add salt. Bring to a boil and simmer until crisp-tender (about 3 minutes). Drain well.

5. Mix soy sauce, water, sugar, and remaining sherry.

6. In a small, heavy saucepan over medium-high heat, heat oil. Add ginger, minced green onion, and garlic; sauté, stirring, for 30 seconds. Add soy sauce mixture and bring to simmer. Pour mixture over fish.

7. Set fish in its plate in steamer top above boiling water and cover tightly. Steam fish over high heat until a cake tester or thin skewer inserted into thickest part of fish comes out hot to touch (about 10 minutes).

8. Remove fish from steamer and scatter carrot and green onion strips over it. Serve on its plate.

Serves 2 as a main course.

HALIBUT FILLETS WITH GARLIC SAUCE AND TOMATOES

A flavorful garlic sauce made quickly in the food processor adds zest to steamed halibut. The sauce is made by the same principles as homemade Mayonnaise (see page 46). If using a small steamer, steam the halibut in two batches so that the pieces form only one layer in the steamer.

> 1½ *pounds halibut fillets, in 4 pieces, about ½ inch thick*
> *Salt and pepper*
> 12 *leaves romaine lettuce, rinsed and dried thoroughly*
> 2 *medium-sized, ripe tomatoes, cut in thin wedges, for garnish*

Garlic Sauce

> 4 *large cloves garlic, peeled*
> 2 *egg yolks, at room temperature*
> 1 *tablespoon plus 1 teaspoon fresh, strained lemon juice*
> 1 *cup olive oil, at room temperature*
> *Salt and pepper*
> 2 *tablespoons warm water*

1. Bring at least 1 inch of water to a boil in base of steamer. Boiling water should not reach holes in top part of steamer.

2. Season halibut pieces lightly with salt and pepper on both sides. Arrange them in one layer in steamer top and set above boiling water. Cover tightly and steam over high heat until fish is just tender and opaque (about 4 minutes). Drain on paper towels. Let cool to room temperature.

3. To serve, make a bed of romaine lettuce on each plate and set halibut on top. Coat halibut with Garlic Sauce and garnish plate with tomato wedges. Serve cold or at room temperature.

Serves 4 as a main course.

Garlic Sauce Turn on food processor and drop garlic through feed tube. Continue processing until garlic is very finely chopped. Add egg yolks, 1 tablespoon of the lemon juice, 1 tablespoon of the oil, and a little salt and pepper and process until thoroughly blended. With machine running, gradually pour in remaining oil in a fine stream. Transfer sauce to a bowl. Gradually whisk in remaining teaspoon lemon juice. Gradually whisk in warm water to make sauce slightly thinner. Taste and add more salt, pepper, and lemon juice, if needed. Sauce can be kept, covered, up to 2 days in refrigerator.

STEAMED MUSSELS WITH SHALLOTS AND CREAM

Mussels are cooked by a combination of poaching and steaming. For this dish, the mussels are served in their shells and accompanied by crusty French or Italian bread for dipping in the sauce. Small clams can be substituted for the mussels. Serve this dish as a first course, followed by Roast Beef With Spring Vegetables (see page 104) or Duck With Madeira and Pears (see page 106).

1½ pounds mussels
½ cup dry white wine
Pinch of dried thyme
2 medium shallots, chopped
½ cup whipping cream
1 tablespoon chopped parsley
Pepper and salt

1. Prepare mussels as described on page 15.

2. Put cleaned mussels in a medium saucepan and add wine, thyme, and shallots. Cover and cook over medium-high heat, shaking pan often, until mussels open (about 5 minutes). Discard any that do not open.

3. Remove mussels from cooking liquid with a slotted spoon, reserving liquid, and transfer them to a deep serving dish. Cover mussels and keep them warm.

4. Leave cooking liquid undisturbed for 10 minutes, then carefully pour it into a strainer lined with several layers of dampened cheesecloth and strain into another medium saucepan, leaving any sand behind.

5. Bring cooking liquid to a boil. Stir in cream. Reduce heat to medium and simmer, stirring often, until sauce is thick enough to coat a spoon (about 4 minutes).

6. Add parsley and pinch of pepper. Taste and add salt and pepper, if needed. Pour sauce over mussels and serve immediately.

Serves 2 as a first course.

STEAMED SPINACH WITH NUTMEG AND CREAM

Steaming is a good technique for cooking spinach because it quickly becomes tender. Serve this delicate side dish with fish, chicken, or veal.

2 pounds fresh spinach
1 tablespoon butter
¼ cup whipping cream
Salt and pepper
Freshly grated nutmeg

1. Bring at least 1 inch of water to a boil in base of steamer. Boiling water should not reach holes in top part of steamer.

2. Discard spinach stems and rinse leaves thoroughly (see page 14). Put leaves in steamer top above boiling water and cover. Steam over high heat, stirring occasionally, until leaves are wilted and just tender (about 8 minutes).

3. Rinse spinach with cold water. Squeeze spinach to remove as much liquid as possible. Chop spinach coarsely with a knife.

4. Melt butter in a medium-sized saucepan over medium heat. Add spinach and cook, stirring, for 2 minutes. Stir in cream, salt, pepper, and nutmeg and cook, stirring, until cream is absorbed. Taste and add more salt, pepper, and nutmeg, if needed.

Serves 4.

STEAMED NEW POTATOES WITH PARSLEY-LEMON BUTTER

Potatoes may be steamed peeled or unpeeled. Unlike many other vegetables, potatoes should always be cooked until very tender; they should not remain crunchy. These potatoes can accompany almost any food, from poached fish to roast or grilled chicken and meat.

1½ pounds new potatoes
Salt

Parsley-Lemon Butter

¼ cup butter, softened
1 teaspoon fresh, strained lemon juice
Salt and pepper
1 tablespoon chopped parsley

1. Use point of vegetable peeler to remove eyes from potatoes. Scrub potatoes well or peel if desired.

2. Make Parsley-Lemon Butter; keep it at room temperature.

3. Bring at least 1 inch of water to a boil in base of steamer. Boiling water should not reach holes in top part of steamer.

4. Set potatoes in steamer top and sprinkle with salt. Cover tightly and steam over high heat until tender when pierced with a sharp knife (about 20 minutes). Remove potatoes, drain briefly on paper towels, and transfer to a serving bowl.

5. Add Parsley-Lemon Butter in spoonfuls and toss lightly with potatoes. Serve immediately.

Serves 4.

Parsley-Lemon Butter Beat butter in medium-sized bowl until very smooth. Gradually beat in lemon juice and season to taste with salt and pepper. Stir in parsley. Parsley-Lemon Butter can be kept, covered, up to 3 days in refrigerator, or frozen.

SCALLOP SALAD WITH RED PEPPERS, BLACK OLIVES, AND OLIVE OIL DRESSING

For this colorful and light salad, the scallops are served warm or at room temperature to keep their flavor as fresh as possible.

1 tablespoon olive oil
1 red bell pepper, cored and
   cut in thin strips
   Salt
¾ pound sea scallops
12 leaves of leaf lettuce (also
   called salad bowl lettuce),
   rinsed and dried thoroughly
   Pepper
½ cup Vinaigrette Dressing (see
   page 49) made with olive oil
½ cup pitted black olives

1. Heat olive oil in a medium frying pan over medium-low heat. Add bell pepper and a pinch of salt and sauté until barely tender (about 3 minutes). Using a slotted spoon, transfer peppers to a plate and reserve at room temperature.

2. Remove small white muscle from side of each scallop. Rinse scallops and dry thoroughly. Refrigerate until ready to use.

3. A short time before serving, tear each lettuce leaf in 2 or 3 pieces and arrange lettuce on 4 plates or on a platter.

4. Bring at least 1 inch of water to a boil in base of steamer. Boiling water should not reach holes in top part of steamer.

5. Season scallops lightly with salt and pepper. Arrange them in one layer in steamer top and set above boiling water. Cover tightly and steam over high heat until just tender and opaque (about 3 minutes). Drain on paper towels.

6. Whisk dressing again to mix it thoroughly and spoon about one third of it over lettuce. Arrange scallops on top of lettuce in a ring and spoon all but 1 tablespoon of remaining dressing over them. Put peppers in center of ring and spoon remaining dressing over them. Set olives around ring of scallops. Serve immediately.

Serves 4 as a first course or 2 as a main course.

Steaming is a wonderful technique for cooking scallops; serve them with either warm sauces such as Beurre Blanc (see page 44) or a cool dressing, as in Scallop Salad With Red Peppers, Black Olives, and Olive Oil Dressing.

For a somewhat unusual salad, try steamed beets dressed with a Dijon mustard vinaigrette; pecans add a crunchy accent.

BEET SALAD WITH PECANS AND MIXED GREENS

Beets keep all their flavor when they are steamed. Their delicate sweetness is a wonderful complement to the slight bitterness of the greens and the sharpness of the mustard dressing.

   5 *small beets (about 1½ inches in diameter)*
   ¾ *pound Belgian endive*
   ½ *cup Thick Mustard Vinaigrette (see page 48)*
  12 *leaves romaine lettuce, rinsed, thoroughly dried, and cut in strips ½ inch wide*
       Salt and pepper
   ½ *cup pecan pieces*

1. Bring at least 1 inch of water to a boil in base of steamer. Boiling water should not reach holes in top part of steamer.

2. Rinse beets, taking care not to pierce the skin. Place beets in steamer top above boiling water. Cover tightly and steam over high heat, adding boiling water occasionally as needed, until beets are tender (about 50 minutes).

3. Remove beets and let cool. Peel beets while holding them under cold running water.

4. Wipe endive and trim bases. Cut leaves in fairly thin slices crosswise. In medium bowl, combine endive with vinaigrette and toss. Leave to marinate for 5 minutes.

5. Just before serving, dice beets and add to endive mixture. Add strips of lettuce and toss gently. Taste and add salt and pepper, if needed. Sprinkle with pecans and serve.

Serves 6.

POACHING

Poaching is gently cooking food in liquid. Although the liquid may be brought to a boil before the food is added, the food is cooked over low heat so that the liquid is hot but not bubbling. Almost any food can be poached, but the technique is particularly suited to fish, whether whole, in fillets, or in steaks; shellfish; and chicken, especially breasts. Beef and pork, especially cuts that require long cooking, can also be poached. Eggs are poached in water and vinegar. Even fruit can be poached in syrup (see page 118).

During poaching, a flavor exchange takes place between the liquid and the food. The liquid adds flavor to the food and in turn gains flavor from it. Chicken stock is the best liquid for poaching chicken, and fish stock or court bouillon are best for poaching seafood. *Court bouillon,* a special poaching liquid used mainly for fish and shellfish, is made from water, wine, aromatic vegetables, and herbs. Although beef stock can be used to poach beef, it is not really necessary because the meat itself turns water into a stock in the relatively long cooking time required for poaching.

Because the poaching liquid gains flavor from the food, it can be used to prepare an accompanying sauce. Court bouillon can be boiled and enriched with cream, as in Lobster With Saffron Sauce and Vegetables (see page 61). Chicken stock can be quickly made into a sauce by the addition of kneaded butter, as in Poached Chicken Breasts With Zucchini and Cilantro (see page 58). Many poaching liquids also make a good soup. Many poaching liquids, such as that used for Provençal Pot au Feu (see page 58), also make a delicious broth.

Before poaching, most foods are seared in a boiling liquid so that they do not lose too much flavor to the liquid. They then are poached over very low heat. Often food is poached in relatively large pieces because they remain more moist than small ones would. Many meats are poached with their bones in because the bones add flavor to both the food and the cooking liquid and help prevent the food from becoming dry.

Any good heavy saucepan that holds the food and enough liquid to cover is suitable for poaching. It is best not to choose too large a pan because too much liquid would be needed to cover the food, and it would lose flavor.

SOLE WITH MUSHROOM SAUCE

Fish fillets can be poached quickly and easily in a combination of white wine and fish stock. In this dish, the cooking liquids of both the sole and the mushrooms are used to prepare a creamy velouté sauce. Fresh chives accent the dish with tiny flecks of bright green.

> ½ *pound mushrooms, cut in thin slices*
> ½ *teaspoon fresh, strained lemon juice*
> *Salt and white pepper*
> 3 *tablespoons butter*
> 1¼ *pounds sole fillets*
> ¼ *cup dry white wine*
> 2 *cups Fish Stock (see page 21)*
> 2 *shallots, finely chopped*
> 2 *tablespoons plus 1 teaspoon flour*
> ½ *cup whipping cream*
> 2 *tablespoons thinly sliced chives*

1. Combine mushrooms, lemon juice, salt, pepper, and 1 tablespoon of the butter in a medium-sized saucepan. Cover and bring to a boil. Cook over medium-high heat until tender (about 3 minutes). Drain mushrooms, reserving liquid.

2. Fold sole fillets in half, with the whiter side outward.

3. Combine white wine, Fish Stock, and shallots in a sauté pan or large saucepan. Bring to a simmer. Add folded fillets and sprinkle them with salt and pepper. Return to a simmer. Cover, reduce heat to low, and cook until fish is opaque and a cake tester or thin skewer inserted into thickest part of fish comes out hot to touch (about 8 minutes).

4. Carefully remove fish from liquid, using two slotted spatulas, and set on paper towels. Transfer carefully to a platter, cover, and keep warm. Strain cooking liquid and reserve.

5. Pour mushroom liquid into measuring cup. Add enough of sole cooking liquid to make 1½ cups. Reserve remaining fish stock for another use.

6. Melt remaining 2 tablespoons butter in a medium-sized, heavy saucepan over low heat. Whisk in flour. Cook, whisking constantly, until mixture turns a light beige color (about 3 minutes). Remove from heat and let cool slightly.

7. Gradually pour measured liquid into flour mixture, whisking. Bring to a boil over medium-high heat, whisking constantly. Reduce heat to medium-low and simmer, uncovered, whisking often, for 5 minutes.

8. Whisk in cream and bring to a boil. Simmer, whisking often, until sauce is thick enough to coat a spoon (about 5 minutes).

9. Add mushrooms to sauce and warm over low heat. Remove from heat and stir in chives. Taste and add more salt and pepper, if needed. Spoon sauce and mushrooms over sole and serve immediately.

Serves 4.

PROVENÇAL POT AU FEU

This French family-style dinner in a pot contains poached beef and a selection of vegetables. Variations are made with pork and sometimes lamb. The cooking broth is served as a first course, followed by a main course of the beef and vegetables, accompanied with Dijon mustard, French pickles called *cornichons*, and coarse salt. Any extra broth can be saved and used as stock. Leftover beef with Vinaigrette Dressing (see page 49) makes a good salad. It is important to cook the beef slowly and evenly. Prolonged boiling toughens the meat and clouds the broth.

    6 marrow bones (about 3 lbs)
    3 cloves garlic, peeled
    1 bay leaf
    ½ teaspoon dried thyme
    3 stems parsley (without leaves)
    2 whole cloves
    5 peppercorns
    1 large onion
    1 stalk celery, halved crosswise
    1 teaspoon salt
    16 cups water
    3 pounds boneless beef chuck,
       in one piece
    4 medium leeks, cleaned
       (see page 11)
    4 medium carrots, halved
       crosswise
    1 medium turnip, peeled and
       cut in 8 wedge-shaped pieces
    1 large tomato, cut in 8 wedges
       Pepper
    12 thin slices of French bread
       (baguette), toasted
       Dijon mustard

1. Put marrow bones on a large piece of cheesecloth, wrap them, and tie them closed with kitchen string. Put garlic, bay leaf, thyme, parsley, cloves, and peppercorns on another piece of cheesecloth, bring corners of cheesecloth together to enclose them, and tie tightly.

2. In stockpot or other large pot (at least 7 quarts), combine marrow bones, cheesecloth bag of seasonings, onion, celery, salt, and water. Bring to a boil.

3. Add beef to pot and bring liquid to a simmer, skimming froth from surface. Cover and cook over low heat, skimming froth and fat occasionally, for 1½ hours. Water should bubble gently; if it boils hard, reduce heat to very low and cover pot only partially.

4. Cut off and discard all but 2 inches of dark green part of leeks. Tie leeks in 2 bundles with string.

5. After beef has cooked for 1½ hours, add carrots, turnip, tomato, and leeks to pot. Push vegetables into liquid. Add just enough water, if necessary, to cover vegetables. Bring to a simmer. Cover and cook until beef and vegetables are tender when pierced with a sharp knife (about 1 more hour). Beef and vegetables can be kept hot in broth for 1 hour. Pot au feu can be kept for 2 days in refrigerator, with broth in one container and beef and vegetables in another; reheat beef and vegetables gently in broth before serving.

6. To serve, remove beef to platter and arrange vegetables around it. Cut strings from leeks. Cover platter and keep warm. Discard celery, onion, and cheesecloth bag of herbs.

7. Strain about 6 cups broth into a medium saucepan. Taste broth and add salt and pepper, if needed.

8. Remove marrow bones and scoop out marrow. Spread marrow on slices of toast. Serve toast with the strained broth as first course. Then serve platter of meat, accompanied with Dijon mustard.

Serves 6.

POACHED CHICKEN BREASTS WITH ZUCCHINI AND CILANTRO

To keep chicken breasts as moist and as flavorful as possible, poach them gently in chicken stock. The skin and bones left intact add flavor and help prevent dryness. Turn the poaching liquid into a light sauce by thickening it with kneaded butter, a mixture of butter and flour that is added directly to the hot liquid. Hot cooked rice makes a good accompaniment.

    3 cups Chicken Stock (see
       page 20)
    ½ cup dry white wine
       Salt
    4 chicken breast halves, with
       bones (about 2¼ lbs total)
    1 medium zucchini
    3 tablespoons whipping cream
    2 tablespoons chopped cilantro
       leaves
       Pepper
    1 tablespoon butter, at room
       temperature, combined with
       2 teaspoons flour

1. Choose a heavy, medium-sized saucepan in which chicken breasts will just fit. (Do not add chicken breasts at this point.) Combine stock, wine, and pinch of salt in saucepan and bring to a boil.

2. Add chicken breasts to saucepan and press them firmly into liquid so that they are just covered. Bring to a boil. Reduce heat to low, cover, and simmer 12 minutes. Turn top chicken pieces over. Cover and continue cooking until chicken is very tender when pierced with a sharp knife and is no longer pink inside (about 8 minutes). Remove chicken from liquid and remove skin. Put chicken on a platter, cover, and keep warm.

3. While the chicken simmers, cut zucchini into strips ¼ inch by ¼ inch and about 1½ inches long. Add zucchini to chicken cooking liquid and cook over medium heat until just tender (about 2 minutes). Remove with slotted spoon.

4. Measure 1 cup of chicken cooking liquid and reserve for sauce. Reserve remaining stock for another use.

5. In a small bowl, mash together butter and flour until blended to a smooth paste. Set aside at room temperature.

6. In a small saucepan over medium-high heat, bring reserved 1 cup liquid to a boil. Whisk in kneaded butter, in two portions. Bring to a boil, whisking.

7. Whisk in cream and bring to a boil. Simmer, whisking occasionally, until sauce is thick enough to coat a spoon. Remove from heat. Whisk in cilantro. Stir in zucchini. Taste and add salt and pepper, if needed.

8. Discard any liquid that has collected in platter. Put chicken pieces on plates and spoon zucchini and sauce over them.

Serves 4.

Cilantro flavors the creamy sauce that tops these poached chicken breasts. Serve them with a fluffy rice pilaf.

59

Serve Lobster With Saffron Sauce and Vegetables for a special occasion, accompanied by fresh crusty bread and a glass of chilled Chardonnay.

LOBSTER WITH SAFFRON SAUCE AND VEGETABLES

Lobster is poached in a large amount of liquid at relatively high heat so that it will cook quickly; the lobster's shell protects its meat from toughening. In this festive dish, the red and white of the lobster meat contrast with the rich yellow of the saffron sauce. The lobster is cooked in a court bouillon, some of which is then made into the sauce. The remaining court bouillon can be used for poaching fish or other shellfish. For a simpler recipe, the lobster can be cooked in salted water instead of court bouillon and accompanied with melted butter.

>   2 live lobsters (1½ lbs each)
>   ¼ teaspoon crumbled saffron
>   threads
>   ¾ cup whipping cream
>   Salt and white pepper

Court Bouillon

> 12 cups water
>   2 medium carrots, quartered
>   lengthwise and cut in thin
>   slices
>   White and light green part of
>   1 leek, cleaned (see page 11),
>   quartered lengthwise, and cut
>   in thin slices
>   2 stalks celery, quartered length-
>   wise and cut in thin slices
>   1 teaspoon salt
>   2 bay leaves
>   ½ teaspoon dried thyme
>   5 stems parsley (without leaves)
>   ¼ teaspoon black peppercorns
> 1½ cups dry white wine

1. Prepare Court Bouillon.

2. Bring Court Bouillon (without reserved vegetables) to a boil in a large saucepan or stockpot. Add one lobster, head first, to Court Bouillon. Bring to a boil. Cover and cook over medium-high heat for 10 minutes.

3. Remove lobster with slotted spoon and put in a large bowl of cold water. Bring Court Bouillon to a boil again and cook second lobster in the same way. Reserve ¾ cup Court Bouillon.

4. When lobsters are cool enough to handle, pull off tails with a twisting motion. To remove tail meat, press on sides of tails with both hands to break bars on undersides of shells. Slip tail meat from shells. Pull off claws and crack them with a lobster cracker or a nutcracker; remove meat, discarding piece of cartilage inside. There is little meat in head and legs, but head can be split in half and some meat removed; to remove meat from legs, use lobster forks or thin skewers. Cut tail meat in 4 or 5 slices and meat of each claw in 2 or 3 pieces.

5. Strain reserved ¾ cup Court Bouillon into a heavy, medium-sized saucepan. Add saffron and boil until liquid is reduced to 2 tablespoons.

6. Stir cream into saffron mixture and bring to a boil. Boil, stirring often, until sauce is thick enough to coat a spoon (about 3 minutes).

7. Add the reserved ¾ cup vegetables from the Court Bouillon to sauce. Add lobster meat and warm over low heat until just hot. Taste and add salt and pepper, if needed.

8. Spoon lobster and vegetables into rimmed plates, letting sauce run to rim of each plate. Serve hot.

Serves 2 as a main course.

Court Bouillon Combine water, carrots, leek, celery, and salt in a large saucepan or stockpot. Put bay leaves, thyme, parsley, and peppercorns on a piece of cheesecloth, bring corners of cheesecloth together to enclose ingredients, and tie tightly. Add to pot. Cover and bring to a boil. Reduce heat to low and simmer for 20 minutes. Remove ¾ cup of the vegetables with a slotted spoon, drain them thoroughly, and reserve. Add wine to mixture in stockpot.

. . . ON POACHING

☐ *Start the poaching process by bringing the liquid to a full rolling boil. Add the food to be poached and return the liquid to a boil. Then reduce the heat immediately. If you let the liquid continue to boil, it will toughen meat and cause fish to fall apart.*

☐ *Do not overcook foods that are being poached. When cooked too long, shellfish becomes tough and rubbery; fish and chicken lose their flavor.*

☐ *Poached fish is very fragile. Use slotted spatulas to remove it carefully from the poaching liquid and handle it as delicately as possible to avoid its falling apart.*

☐ *When poached fish is allowed to stand, it releases liquid onto the platter. This liquid detracts from the finished dish and should be removed. Blot the platter dry with paper towels just before coating the fish with its sauce.*

SHRIMP AND GREEN BEAN SALAD

In this recipe, shrimp are cooked in salted water, which simulates sea water, then sauced with a tangy dressing. Serve the dressing (which is good with almost any cold seafood) separately, so that the brilliant pink shrimp stand out against the background of bright green beans.

*1½ pounds green beans, ends
    removed, broken in 2
    or 3 pieces crosswise*
*1 pound large raw shrimp,
    shelled and deveined
    Salt and pepper*
4 teaspoons white wine vinegar
4 teaspoons salad oil

Yogurt Dressing

½ cup Mayonnaise (see page 46)
¼ cup plain yogurt
1½ teaspoons Dijon mustard
*1½ teaspoons tomato paste
    Salt and pepper*
*2 tablespoons chopped fresh
    basil or parsley*

1. In a large saucepan boil enough lightly salted water to cover beans generously. Add beans and boil, uncovered, until just tender (about 8 minutes). Drain, rinse with cold water, and drain thoroughly.

2. In a large saucepan, bring 4 cups lightly salted water to a simmer. Add shrimp and reduce heat to low. Cover and simmer until shrimp are pink (about 3 minutes). Drain thoroughly.

3. In a small bowl, combine salt, pepper, and vinegar. Stir until salt dissolves. Add oil and beat with a small whisk or fork.

4. Arrange beans on a platter and set shrimp on top. Spoon vinegar mixture over beans and shrimp and leave for 30 minutes to 1 hour at room temperature. Serve Yogurt Dressing in a separate dish.

*Serves 4 as a first course, or
2 as a main course.*

Yogurt Dressing Whisk Mayonnaise with yogurt in bowl until smooth. Whisk in mustard, tomato paste, salt, and pepper. Stir in chopped basil. Taste and add more salt and pepper, if needed.

SMOKED AND FRESH PORK WITH LENTILS AND SAUSAGES

For this country dish, the meats and lentils are cooked separately, then simmered briefly together to blend the flavors. Serve with Dijon mustard or, if desired, a selection of mustards.

*1 pound fresh pork loin, in
    one piece*
*5 cups water
    Salt*
*1 bay leaf
    Half an onion*
½ teaspoon dried thyme
*1 pound smoked pork loin
    chops, about ½ inch thick*
*1 pound cooked Polish
    (kielbasa) sausages
    Pepper*

Cooked Lentils

*1½ cups lentils (about 10 oz)
    Half an onion, coarsely
    chopped*
2 whole cloves
5 stems parsley (without leaves)
¼ teaspoon dried thyme
1 bay leaf
2 cloves garlic, peeled
2 carrots, sliced
5 cups water

1. Prepare Cooked Lentils.

2. In a medium-sized saucepan, combine fresh pork, water, pinch of salt, bay leaf, and onion. Bring to a boil, skimming. Add thyme; reduce heat to low. Cover and poach pork until very tender (about 45 minutes); an instant-read thermometer inserted into center of pork should register 160° F. Remove pork with slotted spoon.

3. Add smoked pork chops to same pan, still containing cooking liquid of fresh pork. Cover and cook over low heat for 15 minutes. Remove chops with slotted spoon.

4. Add sausages to same pan and bring the cooking liquid just to a bare simmer. Cover pan and let stand off heat 10 minutes. Remove sausages with slotted spoon, reserving the cooking liquid.

5. Remove any bones from fresh pork, trim off excess fat, and cut pork in about ½-inch slices. Halve smoked pork chops if they are large. Cut sausages in 3-inch pieces.

6. If necessary, reheat Cooked Lentils in covered saucepan over low heat. Drain. Put fresh pork slices, smoked pork chops, and sausages in large casserole. Cover with lentils. Add ¾ cup pork cooking liquid and shake casserole to distribute liquid. Sprinkle with pepper. Bring to a simmer, cover, and reduce heat to very low. Heat for 15 minutes to blend flavors. Taste lentils and add more salt and pepper, if necessary.

7. Use slotted spoon to transfer meats and lentils to deep serving dish. Add 2 or 3 tablespoons liquid from casserole to moisten lentils. Serve hot.

Serves 4.

Cooked Lentils Sort lentils, discarding any broken ones and any stones. Rinse lentils and drain. Put onion, cloves, parsley, thyme, bay leaf, and garlic on a piece of cheesecloth, bring corners of cheesecloth together to enclose them, and tie tightly. Combine lentils, carrots, and cheesecloth bag in a heavy, medium-sized saucepan. Add water and bring to a boil. Cover and cook over low heat until tender (about 35 minutes). Discard cheesecloth bag. Lentils can be kept in their liquid, covered, for 1 day in refrigerator.

POACHED EGGS WITH HOLLANDAISE SAUCE AND ASPARAGUS TIPS

Eggs with hollandaise sauce are always a hit for brunch. Broccoli florets can replace the asparagus tips if desired. Very fresh eggs are required for poaching. It is best to poach one or two extra eggs in case one breaks.

> *4 cups water*
> *2 tablespoons vinegar*
> *4 to 6 eggs*
> *16 thin asparagus spears*
> *Salt*
> *1 cup Hollandaise Sauce (see page 42)*
> *4 round slices hot, buttered toast*

1. Prepare pan of warm water for keeping sauce warm and bowl of cold water for cooling poached eggs.

2. Bring water and vinegar to a boil in a large, non-aluminum saucepan. Reduce heat to medium-low so that water just simmers. Break an egg into a small cup or ramekin and slide egg into water where it is bubbling. Repeat with remaining eggs. Reduce heat to low and poach eggs, uncovered, for 3 minutes. Lift each egg carefully with slotted spoon and touch it; white should be firm and yolk still soft.

3. Using slotted spoon, carefully transfer eggs to bowl of cold water. When eggs cool, remove from water and trim edges with a knife. Return to cold water. Poached eggs can be kept in bowl of cold water for 2 days in refrigerator.

4. In a medium saucepan boil enough water to cover asparagus generously. Add a pinch of salt. Add asparagus tips and boil, uncovered, until crisp-tender (about 2 minutes). Drain thoroughly and keep warm.

5. Prepare Hollandaise Sauce (see page 42). Set pan of sauce on a rack above a pan of warm water off heat.

6. Reheat eggs by putting them in bowl of warm water for 2 minutes. Remove carefully to paper towels to drain.

7. To serve, set eggs on toast, coat with sauce, and garnish with asparagus tips.

Serves 4.

WHITE BEANS WITH SAUSAGES, TOMATOES, AND FRESH HERBS

Sausages and beans are a frequent combination in many cuisines because the richness and spiciness of the sausages complements both the texture and the mild flavor of the beans.

> *1 pound dried white beans, such as Great Northern beans (about 2⅓ cups)*
> *10 cups water*
> *1 bay leaf*
> *2 whole cloves garlic, peeled*
> *½ teaspoon dried thyme*
> *1 onion, studded with 2 whole cloves*
> *1 carrot*
> *Salt*
> *2 tablespoons butter*
> *1 onion, chopped*
> *2 cloves garlic, minced*
> *2 pounds ripe tomatoes, peeled, seeded, and chopped (see page 13)*
> *2 tablespoons chopped fresh oregano or 2 teaspoons dried*
> *Pepper*
> *¾ pound frankfurters or other medium-sized smoked sausages*
> *1 tablespoon chopped parsley*

1. Sort beans, discarding any broken ones and any stones. In a large bowl soak beans in 7 cups cold water overnight. For a quicker method, cover beans with 7 cups water in a large saucepan, bring to a boil, and boil for 2 minutes; cover and let stand off heat for 1 hour.

2. Rinse beans and drain. Put in a large saucepan and add the 10 cups water.

3. Put bay leaf, the whole garlic cloves, and ¼ teaspoon of the thyme on a piece of cheesecloth, bring corners of cheesecloth together to enclose them, tie tightly, and add to the pan.

4. Add the clove-studded onion and carrot and push them into beans. Cover and bring to a boil. Reduce heat to low and simmer for 30 minutes. Add a pinch of salt and continue simmering, adding hot water if necessary to cover beans, until they are tender (about 1 hour). Discard cheesecloth, carrot, and onion. Beans can be kept in their cooking liquid, covered, for 1 day in refrigerator.

5. Melt butter in a large frying pan over low heat. Add the chopped onion and cook, stirring occasionally, until onion is soft but not browned (about 7 minutes).

6. To pan of onion add the minced garlic, tomatoes, remaining ¼ teaspoon thyme, oregano, salt, and pepper. Cook over medium heat, stirring often, until tomatoes are soft and mixture is thick and dry (about 25 minutes).

7. Cover sausages with water in a medium-sized saucepan and bring just to a simmer. Remove from heat, cover, and let stand for 7 minutes. Drain well.

8. Reheat beans, if necessary, and drain well. Gently mix tomatoes with beans. Add sausages, cover, and warm over very low heat for 5 minutes to blend flavors. Taste bean mixture and add more salt and pepper, if needed. Sprinkle with parsley and serve hot.

Serves 6.

COLD POACHED TROUT WITH TARRAGON–SOUR CREAM SAUCE

In professional kitchens, a fish poacher placed on the stovetop is used to poach whole fish. A convenient substitute for home cooks is a rectangular or oval baking dish placed in the oven. Unlike other foods, whole fish are placed in cool poaching liquid. If they begin poaching in a boiling liquid, they might fall apart. A frequent accompaniment for cold poached fish is thinly sliced cucumbers.

  5 cups water
  1 carrot, sliced
  1 onion, sliced
  1 bay leaf
  ½ teaspoon dried thyme
  5 stems parsley (without leaves)
  7 stems tarragon (without leaves)
  1 teaspoon salt
  ¼ teaspoon black peppercorns
  ½ cup dry white wine
  4 small trout (8 oz each)

Tarragon–Sour Cream Sauce

  ⅔ cup Mayonnaise (see page 46)
  ½ cup sour cream
  ½ teaspoon fresh, strained lemon juice
  2 tablespoons chopped fresh tarragon leaves
  1 tablespoon chopped parsley Salt and pepper
  1 tablespoon water (optional)

1. Prepare a tarragon court bouillon as follows: Combine water, carrot, onion, bay leaf, thyme, parsley, tarragon, salt, and peppercorns in a large saucepan. Cover and bring to a boil. Reduce heat to low and simmer for 20 minutes. Strain into a bowl and add wine. Let cool to room temperature.

2. Preheat oven to 400° F. Use sturdy scissors to snip fins of fish and trim tails straight. Rinse fish inside and out, removing any scales, and pat dry. Leave on heads and tails. Season fish inside and out with salt and pepper.

3. Set fish in one layer in a large, heavy, flameproof baking dish. Pour enough court bouillon over fish to cover and bring to a simmer. Cover dish with foil. Transfer to oven and bake until a cake tester or thin skewer inserted into thickest part of fish comes out hot to touch (about 12 minutes). Uncover fish and let cool in liquid until lukewarm.

4. If tails of fish have adhered to baking dish, loosen them before moving fish. Use two slotted spatulas to transfer fish carefully to plate lined with paper towels.

5. Remove skin of each fish by scraping gently with paring knife; leave skin on head and tail. Let fish cool to room temperature. Fish can be kept, covered, up to 1 day in refrigerator. Prepare Tarragon–Sour Cream Sauce.

6. Set fish on platter. Coat with Tarragon–Sour Cream Sauce, leaving heads and tails showing. Serve any remaining sauce separately.

Serves 4.

Tarragon–Sour Cream Sauce

Whisk Mayonnaise with sour cream in bowl until smooth. Whisk in lemon juice. Stir in chopped tarragon and parsley. Taste; add salt and pepper if needed. If sauce is too thick to coat trout, gradually whisk in the water.

BOILING

Boiling is essential for the cooking of pasta and is a principal cooking technique for most fresh and dried vegetables and for rice. As in poaching, the food is immersed in liquid, but the heat under the pan is maintained at a higher level than for poaching, so the liquid boils continuously while the food cooks. The liquid used is generally salted water, which is usually discarded after the food has been cooked.

The process used in boiling varies according to the food being boiled. Green vegetables are plunged into a large saucepan of boiling salted water and boiled uncovered; this helps them keep their bright green color. Root vegetables and dried beans, by contrast, are started in cold water so that any undesirably strong flavors can gradually escape into the water as it heats. After they are brought to a boil, root and dried vegetables are simmered until tender.

Another form of boiling is blanching. A very brief boiling, blanching is usually a preliminary to some other process. For example, tomatoes are blanched so that they are easy to peel (see page 13); then they can be sautéed or stewed.

No special equipment is required for boiling. However, you do want to use large saucepans for pasta and vegetables; it's important to give the food plenty of room to cook.

It is possible to boil vegetables a day ahead, refrigerate them, and then reheat them in butter (as in Quick Buttered Cabbage, page 67) or in sauce. Remember, however, that vegetables taste best when they are freshly cooked.

RICE WITH PEAS, SWISS CHARD, AND TOASTED ALMONDS

Rice is often cooked like pasta—in a very large pan of boiling salted water. At least four times as much water as rice should be used. Because this method keeps the grains separate, it is excellent for both hot dishes and salads. You can substitute a cup of frozen peas for the fresh ones, but boil the frozen peas for only 3 minutes.

> ¼ cup slivered almonds
> 1 cup long-grain white rice
> 1 small bunch Swiss chard (about 12 oz)
> 1 pound fresh peas (about 1 cup shelled)
> ¼ cup butter
> 3 large cloves garlic, finely chopped
> Salt and pepper

1. Preheat oven to 400° F. Spread almonds in a small baking dish and bake, stirring a few times, until lightly browned (about 7 minutes). Transfer to a plate and let stand at room temperature.

2. In a large saucepan boil enough lightly salted water to cover rice generously. Add rice, stir once, and boil, uncovered, until tender (about 14 minutes); check for doneness by tasting. Drain, rinse with cold water, and leave to drain in strainer for 5 minutes.

3. Pull chard leaves from ribs. Discard ribs and rinse leaves thoroughly. Pile chard leaves, halve them lengthwise and cut them crosswise in strips ½ inch wide.

4. In a medium saucepan boil enough lightly salted water to cover peas generously. Add peas and boil, uncovered, until just tender (about 7 minutes). Drain thoroughly.

5. Melt 2 tablespoons of the butter in a large skillet over medium-high heat. Stir in chard leaves and cook for 1 minute or until leaves wilt. Reduce heat to low, add garlic, and cook until chard leaves are tender (about 2 minutes).

6. Add peas, rice, salt, and pepper to pan of chard. Heat mixture over low heat, tossing lightly with a fork, until hot.

7. Add remaining 2 tablespoons butter. Cover pan and let rice stand until butter melts (about 2 minutes). Toss again lightly. Taste and add more salt and pepper, if needed. Sprinkle with toasted almonds and serve hot.

Serves 4.

In Rice With Peas, Swiss Chard, and Toasted Almonds, green vegetables add fresh color to the rice, and the almonds provide a crunchy finishing touch. Serve the dish with grilled or poached fish, meat, or poultry.

HARD-COOKED EGGS WITH CURRY MAYONNAISE

"Hard-boiled" eggs are actually easiest to make without much boiling. After the eggs come to a boil, let them stand in hot water off the heat until they are firm. Overcooking them can result in a dark ring around the yolks and rubbery whites. Accompany these eggs with crusty French or sourdough bread.

> 4 large eggs
> 12 lettuce leaves, rinsed and dried
> 3 small tomatoes, quartered, or 12 cherry tomatoes, for garnish

Curry Mayonnaise

> 2 teaspoons salad oil
> 1 tablespoon finely chopped white part of green onions
> 1½ teaspoons curry powder
> ¼ cup water
> ¾ cup Mayonnaise (see page 46), at room temperature
> Salt and pepper

1. Put eggs in a small saucepan, cover with cold water, and bring to a rolling boil. Remove from heat, cover, and let stand for 20 minutes. Rinse under cold water until eggs cool to room temperature. They can be kept for 4 hours at room temperature.

2. Tap eggs gently to crack shells all over, and peel them. Rinse if necessary to remove any pieces of shell still stuck to eggs. Halve eggs lengthwise.

3. Arrange bed of lettuce leaves on a platter or individual plates. Set eggs on lettuce, rounded side upward.

4. Coat eggs with Curry Mayonnaise. Garnish platter or plates with tomatoes. Serve any remaining sauce separately.

Serves 8 as a first course, or 4 as a main dish for a light brunch or lunch.

Curry Mayonnaise Heat oil in small saucepan over low heat. Add onion and cook, stirring, until soft (about 10 minutes). Add curry powder and cook 1 minute. Add water and bring to a boil, stirring. Simmer until liquid is reduced to about 2 tablespoons. Transfer to bowl and let cool to room temperature. Gradually whisk curry mixture into Mayonnaise. Taste and add salt and pepper, if needed. Curry Mayonnaise can be kept, covered, for 1 day in refrigerator.

CARROTS IN CREAM SAUCE WITH DILL

Other vegetables, such as peas and cauliflower, are also good when enriched with a cream sauce flavored with fresh herbs. Serve these carrots with roast chicken, veal, or pork.

> 1¾ pounds carrots, cut in medium slices
> 1 cup Basic White Sauce (see page 36)
> 2 tablespoons whipping cream
> 2 tablespoons snipped dill
> Salt and pepper

1. In a medium saucepan cover carrots with salted water. Bring to a boil, cover, and reduce heat to medium-low. Cook until carrots are tender when pierced with a sharp knife (about 10 minutes).

2. Drain carrots, reserving ¼ cup of cooking liquid. Cover carrots to keep them warm.

3. Bring sauce to a simmer in small saucepan, whisking. Gradually whisk in reserved carrot cooking liquid and simmer over medium heat, whisking often, until sauce returns to its original thickness (about 2 minutes). Whisk in cream and simmer for 1 minute.

4. Gently stir in carrots and heat briefly. Stir in dill. Taste and add salt and pepper, if needed. Serve hot.

Serves 6.

BROCCOLI GRATIN

A gratin is a popular way of preparing any vegetable that tastes good with cheese. The vegetable is cooked until tender and then baked with cheese sauce. Gratins can be made with one vegetable or with a mixture of cooked vegetables.

> ¾ pound broccoli
> Salt
> 1 cup Parmesan Cheese Sauce, (see page 37), finished with 1 egg yolk
> 2 tablespoons grated Parmesan cheese

1. Preheat oven to 425° F. Divide broccoli into medium florets. (Reserve stalks for soup.)

2. In a large saucepan boil enough water to cover broccoli generously and add a pinch of salt. Add broccoli and boil, uncovered, until just tender when pierced with a sharp knife (about 5 minutes). Drain broccoli, rinse with cold water, and drain thoroughly.

3. Butter a 4- or 5-cup shallow baking dish. Prepare Parmesan Cheese Sauce.

4. Arrange broccoli in one layer in baking dish. Spoon sauce over broccoli, covering it completely. Sprinkle with cheese. Broccoli can be kept, covered, up to 1 day in refrigerator.

5. Bake until hot (about 5 minutes if broccoli and sauce were hot, or about 15 minutes if they were cold).

6. If surface is not brown by the time mixture is hot, broil for about 1 minute until browned. Serve hot.

Serves 4.

POTATO PURÉE WITH GRUYÈRE CHEESE

Potatoes are best when puréed in a food mill rather than in a food processor. Serve this rich purée with turkey or broiled chicken. It can also be the entrée for a vegetarian meal.

> 1½ pounds white boiling potatoes, peeled and cut in 2 or 3 pieces
> 2 tablespoons unsalted butter
> ⅔ cup whipping cream
> 1½ cups shredded Gruyère cheese (about 5 oz)
>   Salt and white pepper
>   Freshly grated nutmeg

1. Put potatoes in a heavy, medium-sized saucepan and add just enough lightly salted water to cover. Cover, bring to a boil, and reduce heat to medium-low. Simmer until very tender when pierced with a sharp knife (about 25 minutes). Drain thoroughly.

2. Purée potatoes in a food mill and return to saucepan.

3. Add butter and warm over low heat, beating vigorously with a wooden spoon. Gradually stir in cream and heat until it is absorbed. Stir in cheese. Continue to stir over low heat until cheese melts and blends into potatoes. Add salt, pepper, and nutmeg to taste. Potatoes can be kept, covered, for 1 day in refrigerator. Reheat over low heat, stirring. Serve very hot.

Serves 6.

Gratin of Potato Purée Reserve ½ cup of the grated cheese. Spoon hot puréed potatoes into a lightly buttered shallow baking dish and sprinkle with reserved cheese. Broil until cheese browns lightly.

PASTA WITH GARLIC, OLIVE OIL, FRESH TOMATOES, AND BASIL

This colorful pasta dish is very simple to prepare because the sauce does not require cooking. Good-quality olive oil, preferably French or Italian extra-virgin oil, is important for the taste of this dish. If fresh basil is not available, substitute 2 teaspoons dried basil and 2 tablespoons chopped fresh parsley. Serve the pasta as a first course or as an accompaniment to grilled fish or roast chicken.

> ½ pound good-quality fettucine or medium-width pasta, fresh if possible
> 3 tablespoons good-quality olive oil
>   Salt and pepper
>   Freshly grated Parmesan cheese (optional)

Uncooked Tomato Sauce

> 1 pound ripe tomatoes, peeled, seeded, and chopped (see page 13)
>   Salt and pepper
> 2 cloves garlic, minced
> ½ cup good-quality olive oil
> 2 tablespoons chopped fresh basil

1. In a large saucepan, boil enough salted water to cover pasta generously. Add pasta. Lift strands with large fork to be sure they are separate. Cook, uncovered, over high heat until just tender but still *al dente,* or slightly firm to the bite (about 3 minutes for fresh pasta or 7 minutes for commercial pasta); check by tasting.

2. Drain pasta thoroughly and transfer to a large bowl. Add olive oil and toss gently.

3. Add tomato sauce to pasta and toss again. Taste and add salt and pepper, if needed. Serve hot. Pass cheese (if used) separately.

Serves 4.

Uncooked Tomato Sauce Mix tomatoes with salt, pepper, and garlic. Gradually stir in olive oil. Stir in basil. Let sauce stand at room temperature for 1 or 2 hours. Taste and add salt and pepper, if needed.

QUICK BUTTERED CABBAGE

This simple, basic technique is useful for cooking all green vegetables. They should be cooked until tender with just a touch of crispness; the easiest way to check is by tasting. When cooked in this way, cabbage remains bright green and has a delicate flavor. Serve it with any meat or poultry, or even with seafood.

> 1 medium head of green cabbage (about 2 lbs)
> ¼ cup butter
>   Salt and pepper

1. Cut hard core from cabbage and discard. Rinse cabbage and cut it in thin strips.

2. In a large saucepan boil enough lightly salted water to cover cabbage generously. Add cabbage and boil, uncovered, until just tender (about 5 minutes); check by tasting.

3. Drain cabbage, rinse with cold water, and drain thoroughly. Gently squeeze dry in a colander. Cabbage can be kept, covered, for 1 day in refrigerator.

4. Melt butter in a large skillet over medium heat. Add cabbage, salt, and pepper and cook, stirring, until butter is absorbed (about 3 minutes). Taste and add more salt and pepper, if needed.

Serves 4 to 6.

Bubbling hot oil and a light coating combine in sautéing and deep-frying to produce a characteristic crisp, browned exterior and flavorful interior.

Sautéing & Deep-Frying

I n both sautéing and deep-frying, the food is seared by hot fat so that its outer surface browns and forms a light crust, trapping the juices and flavors inside and keeping the food succulent. The techniques differ mainly in the amount of fat used. Many of our favorite foods are produced by one of these methods—for instance, sautéed shrimp (see page 71) and steak (see page 74), fried chicken (see page 80), and French fries (see page 81). Follow the directions given in this chapter to produce light, crisp, absolutely delicious sautéed and deep-fried foods!

PREPARING FOODS FOR FRYING AND SAUTÉING

Food to be fried and sautéed should be dry to prevent steam from forming when it is added to the oil. This is first of all a matter of safety for the cook; moisture that comes in contact with hot fat splatters wildly. In addition, steam prevents the hot oil from sealing the food. Before food is sautéed or deep-fried, it is often dipped in a special coating, which further ensures a dry surface, protects the delicate flesh, and helps prevent sticking. The coating forms a thin crust that provides a crisp contrast to the moist food and contributes greatly to the popularity of fried foods.

Lightly cooked seasonal vegetables and green salads are good partners for fried fish, poultry, and meat. Deep-fried and sautéed foods are rarely served with elaborate garnishes. In this way, they keep their pure and simple character.

SAUTÉING

It is not surprising that sautéing is the favorite technique today for preparing a wide variety of foods, both among home cooks and with chefs of fine restaurants. Sautéing calls for briefly cooking food in a small amount of fat over fairly high heat, thus sealing in its natural taste. The food is cooked in a frying pan without liquid and in most cases is not covered. Sautéing is one of the simplest ways to cook and enables the cook to have an elegant main course, such as Sautéed Steak With Shallots (see page 74), ready in a few minutes.

Meats of the highest quality are most suitable for sautéing. Among the dark meats, thin beef steaks and relatively small lamb chops are ideal because they cook through in the time it takes to brown them. Sautéing is also a favorite way to cook chicken livers or thin slices of calf or beef liver. It is a perfect technique for cooking thin pieces of tender light meats, such as veal chops and scaloppine, chicken breasts, and turkey breast slices.

Often slices of meat or poultry are pounded before being sautéed, as in Chicken Breasts With Tomatoes and Oregano (see page 72). The purpose of flattening is not to tenderize these already tender meats, but rather to make the pieces uniformly thin so they cook quickly and evenly.

Any fish fillet can be sautéed. Try to choose fillets that are relatively firm-fleshed and do not appear to be falling apart. Short fish fillets are easiest to sauté because there is less chance of their breaking when they are turned over or transferred to the serving platter. Cut fillets in half before cooking them if they are too long to be handled easily. Very thin fillets such as sole require only about 2 minutes of sautéing on each side.

Thin fish steaks, up to 1 inch thick, and small whole fish are suitable for sautéing too, as are shrimp and scallops.

Almost any vegetable can be sautéed. Those that are naturally tender, such as peppers, mushrooms, and zucchini, can just be cut into small pieces and sautéed. Others, such as broccoli and cauliflower, should first be cooked in water to soften them slightly. Even some fruit can be sautéed (see page 118). Sautéing is also an ideal method for heating leftovers, such as cooked vegetables, meats, seafood, and rice, because they heat quickly and do not dry out.

Oil, which can withstand relatively high heat without burning, is used for sautéing dark meats, so that they are well seared at a high temperature and acquire a deep brown color. Butter gives a lovely flavor to sautéed foods but tends to burn easily at high temperatures. To give light meats, poultry, and seafood the taste of butter without having it burn, cooks often combine the butter with oil. Vegetables can be sautéed in any type of fat because they do not require high heat. Olive oil can be used when you wish to give sautéed foods a Mediterranean flavor.

To protect the delicate flesh of white meats, poultry, and fish, cooks often flour these foods lightly before sautéing them. Floured meat browns more easily than "naked" meat and has an appetizing appearance. If a nonstick pan is used, these foods can be sautéed without being floured; they will not stick, but they will not brown as well either. Red meats are not floured because their higher fat content helps to keep them from adhering to the pan.

Although the coating has a protective function, it too should be treated with care. Floured food should not be allowed to sit for more than a few minutes because moisture from the food will make the coating gummy. For the same reason, the coated pieces of food should never be piled one on top of the other.

A hot pan is essential for successful sautéing. If the pan is not hot enough, the food will absorb too much oil, stick to the bottom, and begin to stew in its juices. A heavy frying pan (sometimes called a skillet) of good quality is required so that the fat heats evenly and the food cooks without scorching. A wok can be used for sautéing small pieces of food. To turn the food over, use one or even two flat utensils, such as wide, slotted spatulas or pancake turners. A frying screen is useful for covering the pan during sautéing to prevent the fat from splattering.

The pan should be large enough to hold the food easily. If all the pieces do not fit, cook them in batches. If they are too close together, the steam produced during sautéing cannot escape, and the food will not be properly seared. In addition, it is difficult to turn the pieces over if there is very little room between them. Still, it is best not to space the pieces of food very far apart because the fat may burn if large portions of the pan are left uncovered by food.

SHRIMP WITH GARLIC AND CHIVES

Fresh garlic is the most popular flavoring for sautéed shrimp. The chives add color and extra zest. Serve these buttery shrimp with rice and a green vegetable, such as broccoli, green beans, or snow peas.

    1½ pounds large raw shrimp,
         shelled and deveined
     1 tablespoon salad oil
    ¼ cup butter
         Salt and pepper
     1 medium shallot, finely
         chopped
     3 medium cloves garlic, minced
     2 tablespoons finely sliced chives

1. Pat shrimp thoroughly dry with paper towels.

2. Heat oil and 3 tablespoons of the butter in a large frying pan over medium-high heat. Add half the shrimp and sprinkle with salt and pepper. Sauté, tossing often, until shrimp are pink (about 1½ minutes). Transfer to a platter using a slotted spoon. Repeat with remaining shrimp.

3. Add remaining 1 tablespoon butter to pan. Reduce heat to low. Stir in shallot and garlic and cook a few seconds. Return shrimp to pan and add any juices that collected in plate. Cook, tossing often, for 1 minute. Add chives and toss over low heat for a few seconds.

4. Transfer shrimp to a platter, spoon the juices from the pan over them, and serve.

Serves 4.

Shrimp With Garlic and Chives cooks in just a few minutes, for a quick, delicious dinner.

SAUTÉED SEA BASS WITH MUSHROOMS AND WINE VINEGAR

The vinegar gives this sauce a somewhat unusual tartness.

*1½ pounds sea bass fillet
    (about ¾ to 1 inch thick),
    cut in 4 pieces
    Salt and pepper
¼ cup flour
6 tablespoons salad oil
¼ cup walnut oil
2 shallots, finely chopped
6 ounces mushrooms, cut in
    thin slices
2 small cloves garlic, minced
2 tablespoons chopped parsley
2 tablespoons mild white wine
    vinegar (5% acidity)*

1. Sprinkle fish with salt and pepper on both sides. Spread flour on a plate. Lightly coat fish pieces with flour on both sides. Tap them to remove excess flour and arrange them side by side on a plate.

2. Heat salad oil in a large frying pan over medium-high heat. When it is very hot, add fillets. Sauté them until they can be pierced easily with a thin skewer (about 4 minutes on each side). If oil begins to brown, reduce heat to medium. Transfer fish to a platter, arrange pieces side by side, and keep them warm.

3. Discard oil from pan. Add walnut oil to pan and heat it over low heat. Add shallots and cook for 1 minute.

4. Raise heat to medium-high, add mushrooms and garlic, and sauté, tossing often, until just tender (about 2 minutes). Add parsley and toss mixture a few seconds over heat. Taste and add more salt and pepper, if needed. Spoon mixture over fish.

5. Pour vinegar into hot pan off heat, swirl it around pan, and pour it evenly over fish. Serve immediately.

Serves 4.

SAVORY CHICKEN LIVERS WITH ONIONS

Liver and onions are a popular combination in many countries. In this version, the livers are flavored with a Middle Eastern spice mixture. Serve them with rice and green beans or zucchini. If possible, cover the livers with a frying screen during sautéing to prevent splatters.

*5 tablespoons salad oil
2 large onions, thinly sliced
    (about 1¼ lbs)
    Salt and pepper
¾ pound chicken livers
1 teaspoon ground cumin
¼ teaspoon turmeric
¼ teaspoon cayenne pepper*

1. Heat 2 tablespoons of the oil in a large, heavy frying pan over medium heat. Add onions, salt, and pepper and stir until coated. Reduce heat to low, cover, and cook, stirring occasionally, until tender (about 20 minutes). Onions can be kept, covered, up to 2 days in refrigerator.

2. Cut livers in half. Cut out any green spots and discard. Pat livers dry with paper towels.

3. Mix cumin, turmeric, and cayenne. Sprinkle livers evenly with salt and with spice mixture.

4. If necessary, reheat onions in a frying pan over low heat. Raise heat to medium; continue sautéing, uncovered, stirring often, until they are lightly browned. Cover; keep warm.

5. Heat remaining 3 tablespoons oil in a large, heavy frying pan over medium-high heat. Add the livers and sauté until browned (about 3 minutes); turn over and sauté until second side is well browned and tender (about 2½ minutes). To check, cut into one large piece of liver; it should be light pink, not red, inside. Do not overcook, or livers will be dry and tough. Taste and add more salt and pepper, if needed.

6. Spoon livers over or around onions and serve.

Serves 2.

CHICKEN BREASTS WITH TOMATOES AND OREGANO

Boneless chicken breast halves are often pounded so that they can be sautéed quickly and remain moist. Use a flat meat pounder, not one with ridges or pointed edges, which may tear the meat. Many butchers will pound the meat for you. Serve the chicken with sautéed quartered mushrooms and buttered pasta.

*4 boneless chicken breast halves,
    skinned (6 to 7 oz each)
¼ cup flour
    Salt and pepper
2 tablespoons each salad oil
    and butter
⅓ cup dry white wine
1 tablespoon chopped fresh
    oregano or 1 teaspoon dried
    oregano
    Pinch of sugar (optional)*

Quick Tomato Sauce

*2 tablespoons butter
2½ pounds ripe tomatoes, peeled,
    seeded, and chopped
1 bay leaf
    Salt and pepper*

1. Prepare Quick Tomato Sauce. Trim chicken breast halves of fat, cartilage, and tendons. Pound them between pieces of waxed paper to a thickness of ¼ inch. Do not pound too forcefully or the meat may tear. Carefully peel off the paper.

2. Preheat oven to 275° F. Spread flour on a plate. Salt and pepper chicken on both sides. Lightly coat 2 chicken breasts with flour on both sides. Tap to remove excess flour; set them side by side on a plate.

3. Heat oil and butter in a large, heavy frying pan over medium-high heat. Add coated chicken breasts. Sauté chicken until it is browned on bottom (about 2 minutes). Using two wide spatulas, turn chicken over carefully. Sauté until second side is browned and chicken is tender when pierced with a small, sharp knife (about 2 minutes). Transfer breasts to ovenproof platter, placing them side by side; keep warm in oven.

4. Repeat flouring and sautéing with remaining chicken. If fat in pan turns brown during sautéing, reduce heat to medium-low.

5. Discard fat from frying pan. Pour wine into pan, add oregano, and bring to a boil, stirring and scraping to dissolve any brown bits in the pan.

6. Add Quick Tomato Sauce to pan and simmer, stirring, until sauce absorbs the wine (about 2 minutes). Taste and add more salt and pepper, if needed; if sauce is too acid, add a pinch of sugar.

7. To serve, spoon a little sauce on each of 4 plates and spread it to coat bottom of plate. Set chicken breasts on top, letting sauce show. Serve immediately; serve remaining sauce separately.

Serves 4.

Quick Tomato Sauce Melt butter in a medium-sized, heavy frying pan over medium heat. Add tomatoes, bay leaf, salt, and pepper. Cook over medium heat, stirring often, until tomatoes are soft and mixture is thick and smooth (about 20 minutes). Discard bay leaf. Purée tomatoes in a food processor or blender until very smooth.

Chicken breasts, boned and skinned, acquire a delicate browned exterior when lightly floured and sautéed, as in Chicken Breasts With Tomatoes and Oregano. Buttered pasta and poached or sautéed mushrooms make perfect accompaniments.

Deglazing with wine is the secret to savory sauces for sautéed meats, as in Sautéed Steak With Shallots.

3. Remove fat from pan. Add port and brown sauce; bring to a boil, stirring and scraping to dissolve any brown bits. Strain into small pan.

4. Bring sauce to a simmer and remove from heat. Whisk in pieces of butter. Taste and add more salt and pepper, if needed.

5. Discard any liquid that has collected in platter. Spoon a little sauce over each steak. Serve remaining sauce separately.

Serves 4.

SAUTÉED STEAK WITH SHALLOTS

Top loin steaks are sometimes called New York steaks. Other relatively small and very tender steaks, such as rib-eye or tenderloin, are also good in this dish. Accompany it with steamed new potatoes, which complement the creamy shallot sauce.

- 2 *tablespoons butter*
- 6 *medium shallots (about 4 oz), cut in thin slices*
  Salt
- *4 top loin steaks, about ¾ inch thick (about 2 lbs total)*
  Pepper
- 2 *tablespoons salad oil*
- ⅓ *cup dry white wine*
- 1 *cup whipping cream*
- 1 *tablespoon chopped parsley*

1. Melt butter in a medium-sized, heavy saucepan over low heat. Add shallots and a pinch of salt and cook, stirring often, until shallots are very tender (about 10 minutes).

2. Sprinkle steaks lightly with salt and pepper on both sides.

3. Heat oil in a large, heavy frying pan over high heat. Add 2 of the steaks and sauté until well browned on bottom (about 2 minutes). Turn over and sauté until second side is well browned and steak offers little resistance to the touch, about 1 minute for rare meat. Transfer to a platter and keep warm. Reheat oil in pan and sauté remaining steaks.

STEAK WITH PORT SAUCE

Thin steaks are best for sautéing. Tenderloin or top loin steaks can also be used for this dish.

- 4 *rib-eye steaks, about ¾ inch thick (about 2 lbs total)*
  Salt and pepper
- 1 *tablespoon salad oil*
- ¼ *cup port*
- 1 *cup Basic Brown Sauce (see page 39) or Quick Brown Sauce (see page 40)*
- 2 *tablespoons butter, at room temperature, cut in 4 pieces*

1. Sprinkle steaks lightly with salt and pepper on both sides.

2. Heat oil in a large, heavy frying pan over high heat. Add 2 of the steaks and sauté until well browned on bottom (about 2 minutes). Turn over and sauté until second side is well browned and steak offers little resistance to the touch, about 1 minute for rare meat. Transfer to a platter and keep warm. Reheat oil in pan and sauté remaining steaks.

4. Discard fat from frying pan. Add wine and bring to a boil over low heat, stirring and scraping to dissolve any brown bits in the pan. Boil wine until reduced to about 3 tablespoons.

5. Stir in cream and bring to a boil. Add shallots and simmer, stirring, until sauce is thick enough to coat a spoon. Taste and add more salt and pepper, if needed.

6. Discard any liquid that has collected in the platter. Spoon shallot sauce over center of each steak, letting ends of steak show. Sprinkle shallot sauce with parsley.

Serves 4.

SESAME TURKEY STRIPS WITH RED PEPPERS AND SNOW PEAS

Sesame oil and sesame seeds add an exciting flavor to turkey. To prevent dryness, always cook turkey breast slices briefly. Cutting the meat in strips before sautéing enables it to cook as quickly as possible. Serve this colorful dish with rice.

> *2 teaspoons sesame seed*
> *1 pound turkey breast slices, about ¼ inch thick, patted dry*
> *½ pound snow peas (also called Chinese peas)*
> *¾ cup Chicken Stock (see page 20)*
> *1 tablespoon soy sauce*
> *1 teaspoon dry sherry*
> *½ teaspoon sugar*
> *Salt and white pepper*
> *1 teaspoon cornstarch*
> *5 tablespoons salad oil*
> *1 red bell pepper, cored and cut in strips ¾ inch wide*
> *3 green onions, cut in 1-inch pieces*
> *3 tablespoons flour*
> *1 tablespoon sesame oil*

1. Toast sesame seed in a small, heavy frying pan over medium-low heat, stirring and shaking often, until seeds are golden brown (about 3 minutes). Transfer immediately to a small bowl.

2. Cut turkey in strips about ½ inch wide and 1½ inches long.

3. Remove ends and strings from snow peas. In a large saucepan boil enough water to cover snow peas generously. Add snow peas and boil, uncovered, 30 seconds; snow peas should remain crisp. Rinse under cold water and drain well.

4. In a medium bowl stir together stock, soy sauce, sherry, sugar, salt, pepper, and cornstarch.

5. Heat 2 tablespoons of the oil in a large frying pan over medium heat. Add red pepper and green onions and sauté, stirring often, until vegetables are softened but still crunchy (about 2 minutes). Reserve in pan.

6. Sprinkle half the turkey strips with 1½ tablespoons of the flour. Transfer to a strainer and toss to remove excess flour.

7. Heat remaining 3 tablespoons oil in another large frying pan over medium-high heat until very hot. Add floured turkey and toss immediately with slotted spatula to separate the pieces. Sauté turkey, tossing often, until it loses its pink color (about 2 minutes). Remove to a plate with slotted spoon. Flour and sauté remaining turkey. Transfer to plate.

8. Stir stock mixture, add to pan used to sauté turkey, and bring to a simmer, stirring and scraping to dissolve any brown bits in the pan.

9. Add turkey and snow peas to pan of vegetables. Strain stock mixture over turkey and vegetables. Bring to a boil over medium heat, tossing. Simmer until ingredients are lightly coated with sauce (about 2 minutes).

10. Remove from heat and stir in sesame oil. Taste and add more salt and pepper, if needed.

11. Transfer to a serving dish and sprinkle with toasted sesame seeds.

Serves 2 or 3.

DEGLAZING SAUCES

A special type of quick sauce, called a deglazing sauce, is often prepared for sautéed meats and poultry. It is made directly in the pan after the meat has finished cooking and has been removed. Deglazing makes use of the meat juices that caramelize on the bottom of the pan during sautéing. These coagulated meat essences, which look like brown bits in the pan, should not be washed out because they are rich in flavor.

To dissolve these juices, add a small amount of liquid to the pan. The liquid can be red or white wine, wine vinegar, port, stock, citrus juice, or a combination of these. The liquid is then reduced, or boiled until it thickens slightly and its flavor is concentrated. This liquid is the base for a sauce and can be thickened like any sauce; one common way to thicken it is by adding cream and boiling the sauce until it thickens by itself, as in Lamb Chops With Creamy Garlic Sauce and Green Beans (see page 76). A variety of flavorings, from tomatoes and fresh herbs to mustard and soy sauce, can add excitement to deglazing sauces.

LAMB CHOPS WITH CREAMY GARLIC SAUCE AND GREEN BEANS

Lamb should be sautéed only briefly so that it remains juicy and is still pink inside.

  5 *medium cloves garlic, halved*
  1 *bay leaf*
  3 *tablespoons white wine vinegar*
  ⅓ *cup water*
  1 *cup whipping cream*
  ¾ *pound green beans, ends removed, broken in 2 pieces crosswise*
  8 *lamb rib chops (about 1 in. thick), trimmed of excess fat*
     Salt and pepper
  3 *tablespoons salad oil*
  ¼ *cup dry white wine*
     Pinch of cayenne pepper

1. Combine garlic, bay leaf, vinegar, and water in a medium saucepan and bring to a boil. Reduce heat to medium-high and simmer until reduced to about 3 tablespoons. Add ½ cup of the cream and bring to a simmer, stirring. Remove from heat.

2. In a large saucepan boil enough lightly salted water to cover beans generously. Add beans and boil, uncovered, until just tender (about 8 minutes). Drain thoroughly and keep warm.

3. Sprinkle chops lightly with salt and pepper on both sides.

4. Heat oil in a large, heavy frying pan over medium-high heat. Add 4 lamb chops and sauté until well browned on bottom (about 3 minutes). Turn over and sauté until second side is well browned and meat is tender but still pink (about 3 minutes). Transfer to a platter and keep warm. Reheat oil in pan and sauté remaining chops.

5. Discard fat from frying pan. Add wine and bring to a boil over low heat, stirring and scraping to dissolve any brown bits in the pan. Boil wine until reduced to about 3 tablespoons.

6. Strain cream mixture into wine and bring to a boil, stirring. Stir in remaining ½ cup cream and simmer, stirring, until sauce is thick enough to coat a spoon. Add a pinch of cayenne. Taste and add more salt and cayenne, if needed.

7. Discard any liquid that has collected in platter. Put lamb chops on edge of a platter with bones pointing outward and arrange green beans in center. Serve sauce separately.

Serves 4.

VEAL CHOPS WITH MUSTARD AND CREAM

Unlike other meats, veal chops are often covered after preliminary sautéing so that the small amount of steam created in sautéing will keep them moist as they continue cooking.

  3 *tablespoons flour*
  4 *veal chops, ¾ to 1 inch thick*
     Salt and pepper
  2 *tablespoons each salad oil and butter*
  2 *shallots, finely chopped*
  ⅔ *cup dry white wine*
  ¾ *cup whipping cream*
  2 *tablespoons Dijon mustard*
  1 *tablespoon chopped Italian (flat-leaf) parsley or regular parsley (optional)*

1. Spread flour on a plate. Sprinkle veal chops lightly with salt and pepper on both sides. Lightly coat chops with flour on both sides. Tap them to remove excess flour and arrange them side by side on a plate.

2. Heat oil and butter in a large frying pan over medium-high heat. Add veal chops and sauté them until brown on both sides. Reduce heat to low, cover, and continue cooking, turning the chops over occasionally, until they are tender when pierced with a small, sharp knife (about 15 minutes).

3. Transfer chops to a plate. Add shallots and wine to pan and bring to a boil, stirring and scraping to dissolve any brown bits in the pan. Boil until wine is reduced to about ⅓ cup.

4. Stir in cream and bring to a boil. Simmer, stirring, until sauce is thick enough to coat a spoon.

5. Remove sauce from heat and whisk in mustard. Taste and add more salt and pepper, if needed.

6. Return veal chops to sauce, discarding any liquid that has collected in plate, and reheat them over low heat, uncovered. Transfer to a platter, sprinkle with parsley, if desired, and serve.

Serves 4.

SAUTÉED POTATOES WITH WHITE AND GREEN ONIONS

The potatoes and onions are sautéed separately and are heated briefly together. Serve them with sautéed or broiled steaks, lamb chops, chicken, or turkey breasts.

  3 *medium-sized white potatoes (about 1 lb)*
  2 *medium-sized green onions*
  3 *tablespoons salad oil*
  ¼ *cup butter*
  1 *medium onion, cut in thin slices*
     Salt and freshly ground pepper

1. In a medium saucepan cover potatoes with salted water. Bring to a boil, cover, and reduce heat to low. Simmer 10 minutes. Drain thoroughly. Let stand until cool enough to handle. Peel by scraping gently with paring knife. Cut potatoes into ⅜-inch-thick slices.

2. Cut green onions in thin slices, keeping white and green parts separate.

3. In a large, heavy frying pan, heat 1 tablespoon of the oil and 2 tablespoons of the butter over low heat. Add onion and white part of green onions and cook, stirring often, until tender (about 10 minutes).

4. Heat 1 more tablespoon each of oil and butter in another large, heavy frying pan over medium heat. Add enough potato slices to make one layer and sprinkle with salt and pepper. Sauté, shaking pan occasionally, 4 minutes. Turn potatoes over, sprinkle with salt and pepper, and sauté until second side is brown (about 4 minutes). Turn over once again, raise heat to medium-high, and sauté potatoes until tender and golden brown (about 2 minutes). Remove with slotted spatula.

5. Add remaining 1 tablespoon each of oil and remaining butter to skillet, and heat. Sauté remaining potato slices.

6. Add green part of green onions to pan of onion mixture and cook over low heat, stirring often, for 1 minute. Add potatoes, salt, and pepper and sauté over medium heat, tossing carefully, for 2 minutes. Taste and add more salt and pepper, if needed. Serve immediately.

Serves 4.

SAUTÉED RED, YELLOW, AND GREEN PEPPERS WITH THYME

Mixed sautéed peppers are a colorful complement to almost any simply prepared food. They can be served with grilled or sautéed poultry or meat, presented as a beautiful buffet vegetable dish, or used as a filling for omelets. If peppers of all three colors are not available, one or two can be used instead.

> 1 *medium-sized red bell pepper (about 5 oz)*
> 1 *medium-sized green bell pepper (about 5 oz)*
> 1 *medium-sized yellow bell pepper (about 8 oz)*
> 3 *tablespoons olive oil*
> 1½ *teaspoons chopped fresh thyme leaves or ½ teaspoon dried thyme*
> *Salt and pepper*

1. Halve peppers lengthwise, core, and remove ribs. Cut into 1½- by ¼-inch strips.

2. Heat oil in a large skillet over low heat. Add peppers, thyme, salt, and pepper and cook, stirring often, until vegetables are tender but not brown (about 12 minutes). Taste and add more salt and pepper, if needed. Peppers can be kept 2 hours at room temperature or overnight in the refrigerator; reheat over low heat, if desired. Serve hot, warm, or at room temperature.

Serves 4.

Sautéed peppers is one of the quickest and most versatile vegetable dishes. It can be served hot, warm, or at room temperature, and you can use any combination of red, yellow, or green peppers.

... ON SAUTÉING AND DEEP-FRYING

☐ Always prepare all utensils, ingredients, accompaniments, and platters ahead. Once the food has been cooked, serve it promptly.

☐ Handle coated food as little as possible so the coating will not come off.

☐ Fried or sautéed foods can be kept hot in a low oven (about 275° F). Uncoated food should be covered to prevent it from drying out. Coated food should not be covered, however, so the crust will remain crisp.

Deep-frying

Because hot oil is dangerous, it is important to follow a few simple rules for safety.

☐ Give your full attention to the frying; do not leave in the middle to do something else.

☐ Do not fill the pan more than half full of oil.

☐ Be very careful not to allow any liquid to get into the oil because it will splatter violently.

☐ Do not drop ingredients from a height because they will splash hot oil; hold them near the surface of the oil and slide them in gently.

☐ Do not crowd the pan because the oil can bubble up to the top and even overflow.

☐ Regulate the heat as necessary to keep the oil at the specified temperature.

☐ Do not move the deep-fryer when the fat in it is hot.

For best results:

☐ Make sure that food is completely covered with the coating material so that no moist surfaces are exposed to the hot fat.

☐ Food added to the oil brings down its temperature. To avoid lowering the temperature too much, fry the food in batches.

☐ Drain fried foods thoroughly on paper towels before serving.

Sautéing

☐ If possible, bring food to room temperature before sautéing it.

☐ Prepare the ingredients for the deglazing sauce ahead and have them at hand. That way, you will not have to hold the sautéed meat for too long.

☐ To prevent sticking, be sure the fat is hot before you add the food. If you are using a mixture of oil and butter, heat them until the butter has completely melted. When using oil alone, check whether it is hot enough by holding a piece of food with its tip just touching the oil. If it does not begin sizzling immediately, the oil is not hot enough; wait several seconds and check again.

☐ If you are sautéing more than four portions of meat or fish, use several pans to avoid having to hold the cooked food for too long.

☐ When sautéing several batches of food, check between batches to be sure there is always a coating of oil on the bottom of the pan. If necessary, add more oil and heat it to the proper temperature (see above) before sautéing the next batch. If some of the coating has stuck to the pan, scrape it off before adding more food.

☐ Before deglazing a pan, scrape off any large bits of coating that are stuck to it, or else strain the liquid after deglazing.

☐ Sautéed vegetables can be reheated, although they will lose some of their crispness.

SAUTÉED CORN KERNELS WITH PEAS

Although very tender farm-fresh corn can be cooked completely by sautéing, it is best to precook any other corn briefly in water before sautéing to make sure it will be tender. Serve this quick, colorful dish with grilled fish or chicken.

> 2 ears fresh corn, husked and silk carefully removed
> 1 pound fresh peas (about 1 cup shelled) or 1 cup frozen small peas
> 3 tablespoons butter
> ½ teaspoon dried marjoram
> Salt and pepper

1. Holding one ear of corn by its base, cut off about 3 rows of kernels at a time with a sharp knife. Repeat with second ear of corn (you should have about 1⅓ cups kernels).

2. In a medium saucepan boil enough lightly salted water to cover peas generously. Add peas and boil uncovered until barely tender (about 5 minutes for fresh or about 2 minutes for frozen). Drain thoroughly.

3. In the same saucepan boil enough water to cover corn generously. Add corn and boil uncovered for 2 minutes. Drain thoroughly.

4. Melt butter in a heavy, medium-sized frying pan over low heat. Add corn and sauté, stirring occasionally, until just tender (about 10 minutes).

5. Stir in peas, marjoram, salt, and pepper and cook over low heat for 2 minutes. Taste and add more salt and pepper, if needed.

Serves 4.

DEEP-FRYING

Most people love the crunchiness of fried fish, vegetable fritters, and perfect French fries but often hesitate to prepare fried foods at home. Yet this technique is neither complicated nor difficult: There is no need to have a fear of frying. Deep-frying is most suitable for pieces of chicken, seafood, and vegetables. Properly fried food is light and not greasy.

As its name implies, this cooking method involves immersing food in hot deep fat. Plain vegetable oil of a neutral flavor, such as corn oil, peanut oil, or soybean oil, can be used, as can shortening or lard.

Pure, clean oil is crucial for crisp, good-tasting fried foods. The fat used for deep-frying can be saved and used again once or twice, but strain it carefully after use and keep it in a cool place. If it smokes during cooking, however, discard it and start again with fresh oil.

Coating is essential to protect most foods from the sizzling oil surrounding them. There are three basic types of coatings. The simplest one is flour, which forms a thin, crisp crust. In the second type, which adds extra insulation, food is dipped in flour, egg, and bread crumbs, which form a crunchy shield that preserves the moistness of fish, chicken, and turkey breasts. The third alternative is fritter batter, which forms a fluffier coating.

Deep-frying should be done in a special deep-fryer or a heavy, deep saucepan. The pan needs to be sufficiently large that when it holds enough oil to cover the food generously it is no more than half full. It should also be very stable so that there is no danger of its tipping over. A slotted spoon or wire skimmer is best for removing the cooked food from the pan.

Correct temperature is vital for successful deep-frying. If the fat is too hot, the coating may burn before the food is cooked inside. If, however, the fat is not hot enough, the food will absorb too much oil. The most efficient way to ensure that the fat remains at the proper temperature is to use a thermometer.

Deep-fried foods are often served on a platter lined with a doily or napkin. They are not served coated with sauce, which would make the crunchy coating soggy. They can, however, be accompanied by a sauce for dipping.

CHEESE PUFFS

Serve these savory little morsels as appetizers. They are made from choux pastry, the same type of dough used to make cream puffs, and flavored with sharp Cheddar cheese. The eggs in the dough cause it to puff in the hot oil.

½ cup plus 1 tablespoon flour
½ cup water
¼ teaspoon salt
¼ cup unsalted butter, cut
   in pieces
2 eggs
⅓ cup shredded sharp Cheddar
   cheese
   Pinch of freshly grated nutmeg
   Pinch of cayenne pepper
   At least 6 cups salad oil
   (for deep-frying)

1. Read "Tips on Sautéing and Deep-Frying" (page 78) before beginning.

2. Preheat oven to 275° F. Line ovenproof trays with two layers of paper towels. Sift flour onto a piece of waxed paper.

3. Heat water, salt, and butter in a medium saucepan until butter melts. Bring to a boil and remove from heat. Add flour immediately and stir quickly with a wooden spoon until mixture is smooth. Set pan over low heat and beat mixture with spoon for about 30 seconds. Let cool for 2 or 3 minutes.

4. Add 1 egg to mixture and beat it in thoroughly. Beat in second egg. Stir in cheese, nutmeg, and cayenne. Beat until well blended. Taste and add more salt and cayenne, if needed.

5. Heat oil in a deep-fryer or deep heavy saucepan to about 370° F on a frying thermometer. If a thermometer is not available, test by adding a drop of cheese mixture to oil; when oil is hot enough, it should sizzle around the drop.

6. Push about 1 heaping teaspoon of mixture into hot oil with a second teaspoon, giving mixture a rounded shape. Add about 6 more teaspoons of mixture in same way. Do not crowd the pan because the fritters need room to puff.

7. Fry mixture, turning rounds over occasionally, until they are puffed and golden brown on all sides (about 4 minutes). Remove them to prepared trays. Put them in oven with the door slightly open while frying remaining mixture. Serve as soon as possible.

Serves 6.

CRUNCHY FRIED CHICKEN

Chicken breasts are ideal for frying because they cook quickly. Rolling the chicken in flour, egg, and bread crumbs before frying gives a crisp crust. Turkey breast slices, too, are moist and delicious when fried this way. Serve alone or with Fresh Tomato Sauce (see page 41).

¼ cup flour
⅔ cup unseasoned dry bread crumbs
1 egg
1 tablespoon salad oil
4 skinned, boned chicken breast halves (6 oz each)
½ teaspoon ground sage
Salt and pepper
At least 6 cups salad oil (for deep-frying)

1. Read "Tips on Sautéing and Deep-Frying" (page 78) before beginning.

2. Preheat oven to 275° F. Line oven-proof trays with two layers of paper towels. Spread flour on a plate. Spread bread crumbs on a second plate. Beat egg with 1 tablespoon oil in a shallow bowl.

3. Sprinkle chicken with sage, salt, and pepper on both sides. Lightly coat a chicken breast with flour on both sides. Tap it to remove excess flour. Dip chicken breast in egg. Last, dip it in bread crumbs, turning chicken over in the crumbs several times until it is completely covered. Pat and press lightly so crumbs adhere. Transfer to a tray or large plate. Repeat with remaining pieces and arrange them side by side on tray. Handle chicken lightly at all stages so coating does not come off.

4. Refrigerate chicken, uncovered, 15 minutes to set the coating.

5. Heat oil in a deep-fryer or deep, heavy saucepan to about 365° F on a frying thermometer. If a thermometer is not available, test by adding a 1-inch cube of bread to oil; when oil is hot enough, bread should turn golden brown in about 1 minute.

6. Add 2 pieces of chicken to oil and fry until golden brown (about 4 or 5 minutes). Remove them to prepared trays. Put them in oven with the door slightly open while frying remaining chicken pieces. Serve as soon as possible.

Serves 4.

MARINATED FRIED FISH FILLETS

For extra zest, fish can be flavored with a marinade of lemon and herbs before frying. Coating the fish with flour before frying gives it a thin, light crust. For a fluffy coating, fish can be dipped in fritter batter. Serve fried fish with lemon wedges or, if desired, Tartar Sauce With Green Peppercorns (see page 48).

1¼ pounds thin fish fillets, such as red snapper (about ½ in. thick), cut in 8 to 10 pieces
Salt and pepper
½ cup flour
At least 8 cups salad oil (for deep-frying)

Marinade

¼ cup dry white wine
2 tablespoons fresh, strained lemon juice
1 tablespoon olive oil
¼ teaspoon dried thyme
Salt and pepper
2 green onions, sliced
1 clove garlic, crushed with a heavy knife
1 bay leaf

1. Read "Tips on Sautéing and Deep-Frying" (page 78) before beginning.

2. Run your fingers over fish fillets to feel for bones. Remove any bones with tweezers or a small, sharp knife.

3. Arrange fish in a large, shallow bowl and pour Marinade over it. Turn fish to coat pieces thoroughly. Let stand 30 minutes at room temperature, turning once.

4. Preheat oven to 275° F. Line oven-proof trays with a double layer of paper towels.

5. Remove fish from marinade, discarding bay leaf, garlic, and any pieces of onion stuck to fish. Discard marinade. Pat fish dry with paper towels. Sprinkle fish lightly with salt and pepper on both sides.

6. Spread flour on a plate. Coat 3 or 4 fish pieces with flour on all sides. Tap them to remove excess flour and arrange them side by side on a plate.

7. Heat oil in a deep-fryer or deep heavy saucepan to about 375° F on a frying thermometer. If a thermometer is not available, test by adding a 1-inch cube of bread to oil; when oil is hot enough, bread should turn golden brown in about 50 seconds.

8. Add coated fish, taking care not to crowd pieces, and fry until golden brown (about 4 minutes). Remove carefully with slotted spoon to prepared trays. Keep warm in oven with the door slightly open.

9. Reheat oil if necessary. Flour and fry remaining fish, in 1 or 2 batches. Serve hot.

Serves 4.

Marinade Mix wine, lemon juice, olive oil, thyme, pinch of salt, and pepper. Add green onions, garlic, and bay leaf.

FRENCH-FRIED POTATOES

Most types of potatoes can be fried, but russets or baking potatoes are especially suitable because they absorb less oil. Putting the raw potatoes in cold water removes excess starch so they do not stick to one another during frying. Because French fries are best when fried twice, this recipe calls for a first frying at a relatively low temperature followed by a brief second frying at high temperature. This method makes meal preparation easy because after the first frying, the potatoes can stand at room temperature until just before serving.

2 pounds large baking potatoes, peeled
At least 8 cups salad oil (for deep-frying)
Salt

1. Read "Tips on Sautéing and Deep-Frying" (page 78) before beginning.

2. If potatoes are over 4 inches long, halve them crosswise. Cut in lengthwise slices about ⅜ inch wide, then cut each slice in lengthwise strips about ⅜ inch wide. Trim irregular edges. As they are cut, drop potato sticks into a large bowl of cold water.

3. Rinse potatoes and drain well in colander. Using paper towels, thoroughly pat them dry in small batches. This step is very important because the fat will bubble up violently if potatoes are even slightly wet.

4. Line trays with 2 layers of paper towels. Heat oil in a deep-fryer or deep, heavy saucepan to about 340° F on a frying thermometer, or test the oil with a piece of potato; oil should foam up around it.

5. Dip a frying basket or a large skimmer into the hot oil, then put about one third to one half of potatoes in basket or skimmer and carefully lower into hot oil. Do not overfill because the fat that bubbles up vigorously when potatoes are added can be dangerous. If you use a basket, leave it in oil during frying; remove skimmer.

6. Fry potatoes until tender but pale (about 5 minutes). Check by pressing one; it should crush easily. Use slotted skimmer to remove potatoes to towel-lined trays. Reheat oil before adding next batch. Potatoes can be left for a few hours at room temperature.

7. About 10 minutes before serving, heat oil in deep-fryer or deep, heavy saucepan to about 375° F on a frying thermometer. Line more trays with 2 layers of paper towels.

8. Put about half of potatoes carefully in frying basket or large skimmer. Carefully lower into hot oil. Fry until golden brown (about 2 minutes). Lift out basket or remove with skimmer and let drain briefly over pan. Transfer to towel-lined trays. Repeat with remaining potatoes.

9. Sprinkle potatoes with salt and toss gently. Serve immediately.

Serves 4.

French fries are the most popular of all potato dishes. Serve them with a thick grilled steak, or with fried fish in the English tradition to make "fish and chips."

Meat gently braised or stewed with aromatic vegetables and herbs acquires tenderness and flavor during the long, slow simmering.

Braising & Stewing

Primarily methods for preparing meat and poultry, braising and stewing employ long, gentle cooking to produce very tender meats with richly flavored sauces. Braised and stewed dishes are often the major part of a meal because they combine both meat and vegetables. And because they can be prepared ahead, can be left more or less alone, and require little or no last-minute work, they are often the best choice both for everyday meals and for entertaining. Recipes for all types of braises and stews appear in this chapter, along with basic information on these cooking techniques.

SLOW COOKING TECHNIQUES

Braising and stewing, both of which can be regarded as a combination of poaching and sautéing, are primarily techniques for cooking meat or poultry. In these cooking methods, the food is first browned, to give it an appetizing color and to seal in some of its juices. Then it is simmered slowly in liquid until very tender. For braising, the meat is cut in fairly large pieces; for stewing, it is cut in cubes or other relatively small pieces.

The long cooking over low heat causes a wonderful exchange of flavors between the meat, the vegetables, and the cooking liquid. Both types of dishes are perfect for making ahead. The flavors harmonize even better after the meat rests in its sauce overnight.

Braising and stewing are ideal cooking methods to use with inexpensive cuts of meat. The slow cooking in moist heat tenderizes the meat and makes it succulent. Yet economy is not the only reason to prepare braised or stewed dishes. These cuts of meat are most flavorful and produce the best tasting sauces.

As in sautéing, the meat or poultry pieces are first browned in oil, butter, or a mixture of both. Then liquid is added to the pan juices to form the sauce base. This technique is similar to the "deglazing" step in sautéing and roasting (see page 75); even the same types of liquid are used—wine, water, stock, beer, cider, chopped tomatoes, or a combination of these. In braising and stewing, however, the meat is returned to the liquid and finishes cooking in it. Often, stock is not required because the meat adds enough flavor to the liquid, especially in the case of beef, lamb, and chicken.

A variety of herbs—such as thyme, bay leaves, rosemary, basil, and oregano—and spices—such as saffron, cumin, turmeric, coriander, and cinnamon—add liveliness to stews and braised dishes, as do condiments, such as capers and olives. For the assertive tastes of lamb and pork, robust flavorings are best, as in Lamb Curry With Ginger and Coconut Milk (see page 94) and the honey and lemon in Braised Pork With Prunes (see page 87). Veal and chicken, by contrast, are often paired with more delicate herbs, as in Cornish Hens With Mushrooms, Tarragon, and Cream (see page 86). Still, these rules are flexible. The most important principle is to use flavorings with imagination guided by good taste.

Vegetables are added in two stages. Chopped aromatic vegetables, especially onions, carrots, celery, and leeks, are often added from the beginning to flavor the sauce. Garlic is common in braised dishes and stews; its flavor becomes surprisingly subtle after lengthy cooking. Tender vegetables, such as zucchini, peas, and corn, are added later, when the meat is nearly tender, so that they will not be overcooked or crushed.

After the meat is cooked, the sauce can be boiled until it is reduced and thickened, as in Braised Lamb With Rosemary, Corn, Zucchini, and Peppers (see page 88); or it can be thickened lightly with flour, as in Rabbit With Apples, Cider, and Calvados (see page 90).

For even heating, a heavy pan with a tight-fitting cover is important. It can be either a flameproof casserole of enameled cast iron or stainless steel or a Dutch oven. It is best to use a wide pan so that the liquid evaporates and thickens gradually. An oval casserole is ideal for braising because it fits the shape of many types of meat, especially cuts that have been rolled and tied.

BRAISING

Like roasts, braised meats are cooked in one relatively large piece and thus retain much of their flavor. Many meats labeled as "roasts" can be braised. In fact, many of the less tender roasts are better when braised than when roasted, in spite of their name. The best foods for braising are shoulder cuts of beef (often called "chuck"), lamb, veal, and pork. Other good cuts are beef brisket, beef round, beef rump, veal shanks, and lamb shanks. Boneless cuts that are rolled and tied in a neat cylinder are ideal for braising because they are easy to carve. Whole chickens and Cornish hens are also delicious when braised.

Unlike many roasts, braised meats are always cooked until they are well done. Braised meat is sliced and served much as roasts are, often surrounded by the vegetables that cooked with the meat or by vegetables cooked separately.

The braising liquid is the base of a delicious sauce. The liquid often thickens naturally during the long, slow cooking or can be lightly thickened with softened butter mixed with flour, as in Thyme-Scented Chicken With Potatoes, Bacon, and Baby Onions (see page 85). Sauces for braised meats are generally not as thick as those for stews.

THYME-SCENTED CHICKEN WITH POTATOES, BACON, AND BABY ONIONS

The combination of potatoes, bacon, and baby onions is frequently added to braised chicken dishes in French cooking. This dish is often regarded as the symbol of good home cooking.

> 1 *frying chicken (3½ lbs), at room temperature*
> ¼ *pound bacon, preferably thick-sliced, cut crosswise in ¼-inch strips*
> 16 *baby onions, peeled (see page 14)*
> *Salt and pepper*
> 1 *tablespoon salad oil*
> 2 *tablespoons butter, at room temperature*
> 3 *tablespoons dry white wine*
> ¾ *cup Chicken Stock (see page 20)*
> 2 *sprigs fresh thyme or ½ teaspoon dried*
> 6 *medium-sized oval potatoes (about 1½ lbs total), peeled, halved lengthwise, and put in a bowl of cold water*
> 2 *teaspoons flour*

1. Remove neck and giblets from chicken. Pull out fat from inside of chicken on both sides near tail. Cut off tail and wing tips.

2. Heat bacon in a large, heavy, oval casserole over medium-low heat until some fat is rendered. Raise heat to medium-high. Add onions and sauté them with bacon, shaking pan often. When bacon browns, transfer it to paper towels using a slotted spoon. Continue to sauté onions, turning them over carefully, until they are browned on all sides. Transfer to paper towels. Discard all but 1 tablespoon fat from pan.

3. Thoroughly pat chicken dry. Sprinkle it evenly on all sides with salt and pepper.

4. Add oil and 1 tablespoon of the butter to casserole and heat over medium-high heat. When the foam subsides, set chicken in hot fat on its side, so that leg is in contact with fat. Cover pan with large frying screen and brown side of chicken. Using 2 wooden spoons, turn chicken gently onto its breast and brown it. Turn chicken on other leg and brown it. Last, turn chicken on its back and brown it. Remove chicken from casserole.

5. Add wine, Chicken Stock, and thyme to casserole and bring to a boil, stirring to dissolve any brown bits in the pan. Return chicken to casserole, placing it on its back. Reduce heat to low, cover, and simmer for 20 minutes.

6. Meanwhile, trim each potato half to an oval shape, using paring knife to round out any sharp angles. Keep potatoes in bowl of cold water until ready to cook.

7. Put potatoes in large saucepan and cover with fresh water. Bring to a boil. Add salt, cover, and simmer over medium heat until nearly tender, about 10 minutes. Drain thoroughly.

8. While chicken cooks, mash the remaining 1 tablespoon butter in a small bowl with a fork until softened. Mix in flour until mixture becomes a uniform paste.

9. After chicken has simmered 20 minutes, add onions, cover, and continue cooking until chicken juices run clear when thickest part of leg is pierced with a thin skewer (about 25 minutes); if juices are still pink, cook a few more minutes and test again.

10. When chicken is tender, transfer it to a platter with 2 wooden spoons, reserving juices in casserole. Cover chicken with foil and keep it warm. If onions are tender, remove with slotted spoon; if not, cook a few more minutes until tender. Spoon onions into a bowl and add bacon.

11. Bring chicken cooking liquid to a boil. Reduce heat to low. Add potatoes, salt, and pepper; cover. Cook potatoes until they are just tender (about 10 minutes), carefully turning them often. With a slotted spoon, remove potatoes to a dish; keep warm.

12. Skim off as much fat as possible from chicken cooking liquid. Boil liquid until it is reduced to about ¾ cup. Discard thyme sprigs (if used).

13. Pour liquid into a small, heavy saucepan and bring to a simmer. Gradually whisk butter-flour paste into simmering sauce, a small piece at a time, whisking constantly. Bring to a boil, whisking.

14. Return vegetables and bacon to sauce and heat 2 minutes over low heat to blend flavors. Taste and add more salt and pepper, if needed. Discard any liquid that chicken has released onto platter. Spoon sauce and vegetable-bacon mixture around chicken and serve immediately.

15. Serve chicken whole and carve it at the table.

Serves 4.

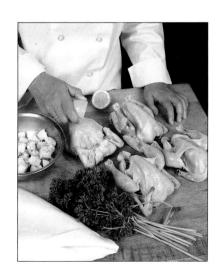

85

CORNISH HENS WITH MUSHROOMS, TARRAGON, AND CREAM

Tarragon is a popular flavoring for sauces for poultry. If desired, use a chicken instead of the Cornish hens and cook it for about 45 minutes after browning. Accompany this dish with pasta to complement the rich, creamy sauce.

- 2 Cornish hens (about 1½ lbs each)
- Salt and pepper
- 2 tablespoons salad oil
- 1 tablespoon butter
- ¼ pound small mushrooms, quartered
- ¼ cup dry white wine
- ¼ cup water
- 5 stems tarragon (without leaves)
- 1 cup whipping cream
- 1 tablespoon chopped fresh tarragon leaves

1. Thoroughly pat hens dry. Sprinkle hens evenly on all sides with salt and pepper.

2. Heat oil and butter in a large, heavy, oval casserole over medium-high heat. Add hens and brown them on all sides. Remove hens to a plate, using 2 slotted spatulas or wooden spoons.

3. Add mushrooms to pan and sauté over medium-high heat until lightly browned (about 3 minutes). Remove to a bowl with a slotted spoon.

4. Return hens to pan, on their backs, and add any juices from plate. Add wine, water, and tarragon stems and bring to a boil, stirring to dissolve any brown bits in the pan. Reduce heat to low, cover, and simmer until juices run clear when thickest part of leg is pierced with a thin skewer (about 35 minutes); if juices are still pink, simmer a few more minutes and test again.

5. When hens are tender, transfer them to a platter with 2 wooden spoons, reserving juices in casserole. Cover hens with foil; keep warm.

6. Skim as much fat as possible from cooking liquid and strain liquid into a large saucepan. Bring to a boil. Add reserved mushrooms, stir in cream, and bring to a boil, stirring. Reduce heat to medium-high and simmer, stirring, until sauce is thick enough to coat a spoon. Add chopped tarragon. Taste and add more salt and pepper, if needed.

7. Discard any liquid that hens have released onto platter. Serve hens whole and carve them at the table. Serve sauce with mushrooms separately.

Serves 4.

BRAISED BEEF WITH OLIVES AND CAPERS

Pasta or rice makes a good accompaniment for this zesty Mediterranean-style dish. Serve it also with some briefly cooked green beans or zucchini. Taste before adding any salt; the olives and capers usually add enough.

- 1 beef chuck roast (2¼ to 2½ lbs), rolled and tied
- 3 tablespoons olive oil
- 8 medium cloves garlic, chopped
- 1½ pounds ripe tomatoes, peeled, seeded, and chopped (see page 13)
- ½ teaspoon dried oregano
- 1 bay leaf
- 2 tablespoons tomato paste
- 1¼ cups water
- 4 tablespoons capers, lightly rinsed and drained
- 1⅔ cups pitted black olives (6-oz can)
- Salt (optional) and pepper

1. Pat meat dry. In a heavy casserole heat oil over medium-high heat. Add beef and brown on all sides. Remove beef to a plate, using 2 slotted spatulas or wooden spoons. Discard all but 1 tablespoon oil from casserole.

2. Add garlic to casserole and cook over low heat for 30 seconds, stirring. Add tomatoes, oregano, and bay leaf and bring to a boil, stirring. Add tomato paste and ¼ cup of the water and bring to a boil, stirring to dissolve any brown bits in the pan.

3. Return beef to casserole with any juices that have accumulated on plate, add the remaining 1 cup water, and bring to a boil. Reduce heat to low, cover, and cook, stirring sauce occasionally, for 2 hours.

4. Add 3 tablespoons of the capers and simmer until beef is very tender (about 1 hour). Remove meat to a platter with 2 wooden spoons. Skim as much fat as possible from cooking liquid.

5. Boil liquid over high heat, stirring often, until it thickens slightly (about 7 minutes). Discard bay leaf.

6. Meanwhile, transfer meat to a carving board and discard strings. Cut in slices about ¾ inch thick.

7. Reduce heat to low. Add olives to sauce and heat, uncovered, for 3 minutes. Stir the remaining tablespoon of capers into sauce and add pepper. Taste and add more salt and pepper, if needed. Beef can be kept, covered, up to 2 days in refrigerator.

8. Return meat slices carefully to casserole, cover, and reheat over low heat. Serve from casserole or from a deep serving dish.

Serves 4.

BRAISED PORK WITH PRUNES

Rice and boiled carrots are a good accompaniment for this dish because they complement the honey-lemon sauce and the prune garnish.

  1 *boneless pork loin roast or shoulder roast (2½ lbs), rolled and tied*
     Salt and pepper
  2 *tablespoons salad oil*
  1 *tablespoon butter*
  2 *medium onions, finely chopped*
  1 *cinnamon stick (2 in.)*
  1 *cup Chicken Stock (see page 20)*
  ½ *cup water*
  1 *cup pitted prunes*
  2 *tablespoons mild honey*
  2 *teaspoons fresh, strained lemon juice*

1. Pat meat dry. Season on all sides with salt and pepper.

2. In a heavy casserole heat oil and butter over medium-high heat. Add pork and brown on all sides. Remove pork to a plate, using 2 slotted spatulas or wooden spoons.

3. Reduce heat to low, stir in onions, and cook, stirring occasionally, until softened (about 5 minutes).

4. Return pork to pan and add any juices from plate. Add cinnamon, stock, and water to casserole, pushing cinnamon stick into liquid. Bring liquid to a boil. Reduce heat to low, cover, and simmer, turning pork over from time to time, for 1 hour and 30 minutes.

5. Add prunes to liquid, cover, and cook until meat is very tender when pierced with a knife (meat should register an internal temperature of 170° F on a meat thermometer) and prunes are tender (about 30 minutes).

6. Stir honey into pork cooking liquid and cook, uncovered, over low heat, basting pork often, for 5 minutes. Transfer meat to a plate with 2 wooden spoons, leaving as much of chopped onions as possible in casserole. Remove prunes to a bowl with a slotted spoon.

7. Skim as much fat as possible from cooking liquid. Boil liquid over high heat, stirring often, until it thickens (about 5 minutes).

8. Transfer pork to a carving board and discard strings. Cut pork in slices about ½-inch thick.

9. When sauce is thick enough, add lemon juice. Taste and add more salt and pepper, if needed. Discard cinnamon stick.

10. Return prunes to casserole and reheat over low heat. Set pork slices gently on top, cover, and reheat over low heat for 5 minutes. Pork can be kept, covered, up to 2 days in refrigerator; reheat pork and prunes in sauce over low heat, covered.

11. Arrange pork slices on a platter or on plates and spoon sauce and prunes over and around slices.

Serves 4 to 5.

In Braised Pork With Prunes, a favorite in much of Europe, the sweetness of the prunes is a perfect accompaniment to the richness of the meat. It is best served with a simple side dish such as white rice or steamed potatoes.

... ON BRAISING AND STEWING

□ Pat meat dry before browning so that the fat will not splatter.

□ While meat or chicken is browning, the fat in the pan may brown. This is all right, but do not let it burn. If the fat begins to turn dark brown, reduce the heat. If the fat is nearly black by the time the meat has browned, discard the fat and add new fat if needed before continuing.

□ To brown, meat needs to stick slightly to the pan so that its juices can caramelize. Do not move the meat around too much or stir it too often during browning because stirring inhibits the caramelizing process.

□ A frying screen is useful for covering the pan while food is being browned because the fat tends to splatter no matter how carefully the pieces are dried.

□ After the liquid is added, the meat or poultry can be braised or stewed in a 350° F oven instead of on top of the stove.

□ Prolonged boiling toughens meat. Once the liquid has been added, bring it just to a boil. Then regulate the heat so that the liquid bubbles gently for the rest of the cooking time.

□ Chicken, lamb, and beef release a considerable amount of fat during cooking. Skim the fat from the surface of the cooking liquid thoroughly before thickening it to finish the sauce.

□ If the sauce of a stew or braised dish is not thick enough, remove the meat and vegetables with a slotted spoon, boil the liquid until it thickens, and then return the meat and vegetables to the casserole.

Braising

□ For braising, brown meats on each side for about 2 minutes over medium-high heat or about 1½ minutes over high heat.

□ To brown the narrow ends of a cut of meat, turn the narrow end down onto the bottom of the pan and lean the rest of the piece against the side of the casserole so that it will not fall over.

□ When turning over a large piece of meat during browning, use two long-handled wooden spoons or slotted spatulas to avoid tearing the meat; stand back to avoid splatters.

Stewing

□ When preparing fish for stewing, do not cut it into pieces so small that they will fall apart.

□ When browning meat or poultry for a stew, avoid crowding the pan or the meat will steam instead of browning.

□ When the meat in a stew is nearly tender, stir it sparingly and gently so the chunks of meat will not break up.

□ Often a stew is thicker the day after it is made because some of the liquid has been absorbed. If the sauce has already reached the desired consistency, it may be necessary to add a little water when reheating the dish.

BRAISED LAMB WITH ROSEMARY, CORN, ZUCCHINI, AND PEPPERS

This colorful dish is very easy to prepare with lamb that is trimmed, rolled, and tied by the butcher. The vegetables are added toward the end of the cooking time so that they keep their flavor, texture, and color.

1 boneless lamb shoulder roast (2½ lbs), trimmed of excess fat, rolled, and tied
Salt and pepper
2 tablespoons olive oil
2 medium cloves garlic, chopped
2 pounds ripe tomatoes, peeled, seeded, and chopped (see page 13)
1 tablespoon fresh rosemary leaves, minced, or 1 teaspoon crumbled, dried rosemary
1 cup water
1 medium-sized red bell pepper
2 ears fresh corn, husked, silk removed carefully
2 small zucchini (6 oz total), cut in ¼-inch slices

1. Pat meat dry. Season on all sides with salt and pepper.

2. In a heavy casserole heat oil over medium-high heat. Add lamb and brown on all sides. Remove lamb to a plate, using 2 wooden spoons.

3. Discard all but 1 tablespoon oil from casserole. Add garlic and cook over low heat, stirring, for a few seconds. Add tomatoes and rosemary and bring to a boil, stirring to dissolve any brown bits in the pan.

4. Return lamb to casserole with any juices from plate and add water. Bring to a boil. Reduce heat to low, cover, and simmer for 1 hour, turning meat over occasionally.

5. Meanwhile, broil pepper about 2 inches from flame, turning it often, until skin is blistered all over (about 12 minutes). Put in a plastic bag, close bag, and let stand for 15 minutes (the steam generated will loosen the skin, making it easier to peel). Peel pepper with a paring knife, core, and drain in a colander for 10 minutes. Cut pepper in ½-inch dice.

6. After meat has cooked for 1 hour, stir pepper dice into meat cooking liquid. Cover and continue to simmer until meat is very tender when pierced with a sharp knife (about 1 hour). Remove meat to a platter with 2 wooden spoons. Skim off as much fat as possible from cooking liquid.

7. Holding one end of a corn cob, cut off about 3 rows of kernels at a time, using a sharp knife. Repeat with second ear of corn.

8. Add corn to casserole and bring to a boil. Reduce heat to low and simmer, uncovered, until corn is just tender (about 20 minutes). Add zucchini and cook until it is tender (about 7 minutes). Remove vegetables with a slotted spoon.

9. Boil cooking liquid for 5 minutes to thicken it slightly. Return vegetables to liquid. Taste and add more salt and pepper, if needed.

10. Meanwhile, transfer meat to a carving board and discard strings. Cut in slices about ¾-inch thick. Lamb can be kept, covered, up to 2 days in refrigerator.

11. Return meat slices carefully to casserole, cover, and reheat briefly over low heat. To serve, set a meat slice on each plate and spoon vegetables and cooking liquid over and around it.

Serves 4 to 5.

Braised Lamb With Rosemary, Corn, Zucchini, and Peppers is a meal in one dish. All that is needed to complete the menu is a simple salad and a light fruit dessert.

89

STEWING

Even more than braising, stewing is a perfect cooking technique for low-priced cuts of meat that would often remain tough if cooked by other methods. A choice cut, by contrast, would probably dry out during the prolonged cooking. Stewing is also good for small bits of meat that are not large enough to roll and would not make neat slices. Other meats suitable for stewing are the same cuts of lamb, beef, veal, and pork that are used for braising, cut into small pieces. Even bony pieces, such as breast cuts, can be added to stews along with meatier pieces; they'll give extra flavor to the sauce. Meat labeled simply "stew meat," which is often a mixture of cuts, can also be used, as can chicken pieces and turkey parts, especially drumsticks and wings.

Seafood stews are made by a different technique than meat and poultry stews and are actually mixtures of seafood that are gently cooked together. Seafood is not browned before cooking. Unlike meat stews, seafood stews have a short cooking time. Any type of seafood can be used.

Vegetable stews may or may not involve preliminary sautéing of the vegetables before they continue cooking in liquid. As with seafood, any vegetable can be part of a stew as long as its cooking time is taken into account. Stewed vegetables are often cooked until very tender rather than crisp-tender as when they are boiled or steamed.

The smaller pieces of meat make a sauce even more flavorful than one made from braising liquid. The stew meat, in turn, gains extra flavor from the sauce. The sauce can vary in consistency, and in many cases there is no need for it to be so thick that it clings to the meat. If there is a generous amount of sauce, it can be used to moisten potatoes, rice, or pasta served as an accompaniment, or each diner can dip pieces of crusty bread into the sauce. Stews can be served from the casserole, in a bowl, or in individual shallow bowls.

The same type of casserole used for braising is appropriate for stewing meats. For chicken, seafood, and vegetable stews, it is better to use a large, deep, heavy frying pan or sauté pan with a tight cover. The larger surface area of such pans promotes evaporation of the liquid.

RABBIT WITH APPLES, CIDER, AND CALVADOS

If rabbit is not available, this stew can be prepared with chicken pieces. Either Golden Delicious or tart apples can be used.

> 1 rabbit (about 2½ lbs), cut in 8 pieces
> Salt and pepper
> 1 tablespoon salad oil
> 5 tablespoons butter
> 3 medium-sized apples (total about 1 lb)
> 1 cup hard cider
> ½ cup Chicken Stock (see page 20) or water
> 3 tablespoons Calvados (apple brandy)
> 2 tablespoons flour
> ½ cup whipping cream

1. Preheat oven to 275° F. Pat rabbit pieces dry. Sprinkle them with salt and pepper.

2. Heat oil and 1 tablespoon of the butter in a large, heavy frying pan over medium heat. Add enough rabbit pieces to make one layer in pan and brown them on all sides. Transfer to a plate. Repeat with other pieces.

3. Peel and dice 1 of the apples and add to pan. Return rabbit pieces to pan and add any juices from plate. Add cider, stock, and 2 tablespoons of the Calvados; bring to a boil. Reduce heat to low, cover, and cook until pieces are tender when pierced with a knife (about 35 minutes).

4. While rabbit is cooking, peel the remaining 2 apples and cut each in 8 wedges. Melt 2 tablespoons more butter in a frying pan over medium-high heat. Add apple wedges and sauté them until lightly browned on both sides and just tender (about 7 minutes). Remove from heat.

5. When rabbit pieces are tender, remove them to a platter using a slotted spoon. Arrange apple wedges around rabbit, cover platter, and keep warm in oven. Skim excess fat from rabbit cooking liquid. Strain liquid, pressing on apple pieces.

6. Melt the remaining 2 tablespoons butter in a medium-sized, heavy saucepan over low heat. Whisk in flour. Cook, whisking constantly, until mixture turns a light beige color (about 3 minutes). Remove from heat and let cool slightly.

7. Gradually pour rabbit cooking liquid into flour mixture, whisking. Bring to a boil over medium-high heat, whisking constantly. Reduce heat to medium-low and simmer, uncovered, whisking often, for 7 minutes.

8. Add cream to sauce, whisking, and bring to a boil. Reduce heat to medium and simmer, whisking often, until thick enough to coat a spoon (about 7 minutes). Add the remaining tablespoon of Calvados. Taste, and add more salt and pepper, if needed.

9. To serve, spoon enough sauce over rabbit pieces to coat them; do not cover apples with sauce. Serve remaining sauce separately.

Serves 4.

EGGPLANT STEW WITH TOMATOES, PEPPERS, AND OLIVES

Stews of eggplant, tomatoes, peppers, and onions are popular throughout southern Europe and North Africa. Unlike other vegetable dishes, these should be cooked until they are very tender. Serve this stew hot or cold, as an accompaniment for meats or poultry, or as a first course. It also makes a colorful addition to a buffet-style luncheon or dinner.

> 5 tablespoons olive oil
> 2 medium onions, sliced
> 1 large clove garlic, minced
> 1 large eggplant (about 1¼ lb), peeled and cut in ¾-inch cubes
> 2 red bell peppers, halved, cored, and cut in thin strips
> 2 green bell peppers, halved, cored, and cut in thin strips
> 2½ pounds ripe tomatoes, peeled, seeded, and diced (see page 13)
> Salt and pepper
> ½ cup whole green olives, pitted
> ½ cup black olives
> 1 tablespoon chopped parsley

1. Heat oil in a large casserole over low heat. Add onions and cook, stirring often, until soft but not browned (about 7 minutes). Stir in garlic and cook a few seconds.

2. Add eggplant and peppers and sauté, stirring, for 5 minutes.

3. Stir in tomatoes, salt, and pepper and bring to a boil. Reduce heat to low, cover tightly, and cook, stirring often, until vegetables are tender (about 30 minutes).

4. Raise heat to medium and cook, uncovered, until mixture is thick but not dry. Add olives and cook for 3 minutes. Taste and add more salt and pepper, if needed. Stew can be kept, covered, up to 3 days in refrigerator.

5. Sprinkle with parsley before serving hot or cold in a shallow bowl or gratin dish.

Serves 4.

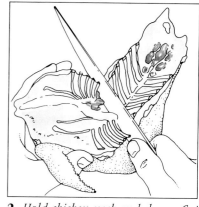

HOW TO CUT UP CHICKEN FOR STEWS

This method of cutting chicken yields 10 small pieces, which will serve 4 people, with a piece of dark meat and a piece of light meat in each serving.

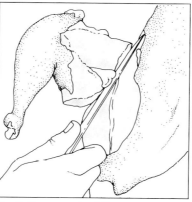

1. Follow step 1 of "How to Prepare Whole Poultry for Roasting or Poaching," page 15. With a large knife, cut off wing tips. Reserve them, with neck, for adding flavor to sauce or save for making Chicken Stock (see page 20). Using a boning knife or other sharp knife, cut skin between leg and body. Pull leg back until joint attaching it to body is visible. Remove leg by cutting through joint, then along body to separate rest of leg meat. Repeat with other leg. Move drumstick in order to feel joint between it and thigh. Cut each leg piece in two by cutting through this joint.

2. Hold chicken neck end down. Cut back from breast along edge of rib cage; ribs should remain attached to back. Use a heavy knife or poultry shears to separate back from breast at neck end.

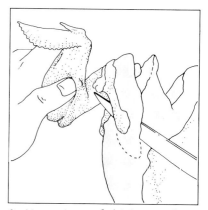

3. Move wing to feel joint attaching it to body. With boning knife, cut through joint; along with wing, cut a lengthwise strip from the edge of breast, so this strip remains attached to wing. Repeat with other wing.

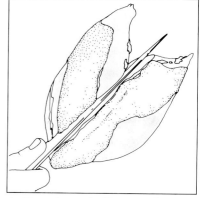

4. Use a heavy knife or poultry shears to cut breast section in half crosswise. If any small sharp bones protrude from breast meat, cut them off with poultry shears; discard. Crack back section in half. Cook with the stew to add flavor, or reserve for making stock.

Stewing is one of the best techniques for cooking beef because it produces a delicious sauce while tenderizing the meat, as in Beef Stew With Red Wine, Carrots, and Shallots. Serve noodles or potatoes on the side to accompany the beef and its sauce.

BEEF STEW WITH RED WINE, CARROTS, AND SHALLOTS

For this stew, the beef is first marinated in red wine with herbs so that it absorbs more of the flavor of the sauce. To save time, however, the marinating step can be skipped and the marinating ingredients simply used as a cooking liquid for the beef.

> 2 *pounds beef shoulder, trimmed and cut in 1½-inch cubes*
> 1½ *cups dry red wine*
> ½ *teaspoon dried thyme, crumbled*
> 1 *bay leaf*
> 6 *stems parsley*
> 1 *tablespoon salad oil*
> 3 *tablespoons butter*
> ¼ *pound shallots (about 6 medium), halved and sliced*
> 2 *tablespoons brandy*
> ½ *cup water*
> *Salt and pepper*
> 1 *pound carrots, cut in ¾-inch slices*
> *Pinch sugar (optional)*

1. Marinate beef: put it in a bowl, add wine, thyme, and bay leaf, cover, and let stand in refrigerator for at least 4 or as many as 12 hours.

2. Remove beef from marinade, reserving marinade, and pat beef dry. Remove bay leaf from marinade; tie it and parsley in a cheesecloth bag.

3. In a heavy casserole over medium-high heat, heat oil and 1 tablespoon of the butter. Add enough beef cubes to make one layer and brown them. With a slotted spoon, remove cubes to a plate; repeat with remaining cubes.

4. Add the remaining butter to casserole and heat it. Add shallots and cook over low heat, stirring, until softened (about 5 minutes).

5. Return beef to casserole and add any juices from plate. Pour brandy over beef, stir, and bring to a boil. Add wine marinade and bring to a boil. Add water, cheesecloth bag, salt, and pepper and bring to a boil. Reduce heat to low, cover, and simmer, stirring occasionally, for 1 hour.

6. Add carrots to casserole and simmer until beef and carrots are very tender (about 3 hours). Remove meat and carrots with a slotted spoon. Skim excess fat from cooking liquid, if desired.

7. Boil sauce, stirring occasionally, until it thickens slightly. Discard cheesecloth bag. Reduce heat to low, return meat and carrots to sauce, and heat gently. Stew can be stored, covered, up to 2 days in refrigerator; reheat it in covered casserole over low heat.

8. Taste and add more salt and pepper and a pinch of sugar, if needed. Serve hot from the casserole or from a deep serving dish.

Serves 4.

CARROT AND BABY ONION STEW WITH RAISINS

The raisins and white wine give this vegetable stew a delicate, sweet-and-sour flavor. When the vegetables are tender, their cooking liquid becomes a buttery glaze. Serve this stew as an accompaniment to any roast or broiled meat or poultry, especially beef, pork, chicken, and duck.

> ¼ cup butter
> 1 pound carrots, quartered and cut in 2-inch pieces
> ½ pound baby onions, peeled (see page 14)
> ½ cup dark raisins
> ⅓ cup dry white wine
> ⅓ cup water
> Salt and pepper
> 1 bay leaf

1. Melt butter in a large frying pan over medium heat. Add carrots and onions and sauté until lightly browned.

2. Add raisins, wine, water, salt, pepper, and bay leaf and bring to a boil. Reduce heat to low, cover, and simmer, stirring occasionally, until vegetables are tender (about 35 minutes).

3. Raise heat to medium, uncover, and cook until the liquid forms a syrupy glaze (about 10 minutes). If mixture is too watery and vegetables are beginning to fall apart, remove them carefully with a slotted spoon and boil the liquid until it thickens; return vegetables to liquid and heat gently. Stew can be kept, covered, up to 2 days in refrigerator; reheat in covered frying pan over low heat.

4. Taste and add more salt and pepper, if needed. Serve hot.

Serves 4.

SHRIMP, MUSSEL, AND CLAM STEW WITH FRESH HERBS

For this stew, the shellfish are cooked separately, then heated briefly together at the end. The clams and mussels are served in their shells, but if you prefer, you can shell the mollusks and serve the whole mixture on a bed of fresh, buttered pasta.

> 2 tablespoons olive oil
> 1 small onion, chopped
> 1 clove garlic, chopped
> 2 pounds ripe tomatoes, peeled, seeded, and chopped (see page 13)
> ½ cup dry white wine
> ¼ teaspoon dried thyme
> 1 bay leaf
> Pinch pepper
> 1 pound fresh mussels in their shells
> 1 pound fresh small clams, such as littleneck or cherrystone, in their shells
> ¼ cup water
> ¾ pound medium shrimp, shelled and deveined (see page 15)
> 1 tablespoon chopped parsley
> 1 tablespoon chopped fresh tarragon
> 1 tablespoon thinly sliced chives (optional)
> 3 tablespoons butter

1. Heat olive oil in a large, heavy frying pan over low heat. Add onion and cook, stirring often, until soft but not browned. Stir in garlic and cook for 30 seconds.

2. Add tomatoes, raise heat to medium-high, and cook, stirring, for 2 minutes. Pour in ¼ cup of the wine and add thyme, bay leaf, and pepper. Cook, stirring often, for 15 minutes. Discard bay leaf.

3. Prepare mussels and clams (see page 15). Discard any mussels that do not close when tapped.

4. Put cleaned mussels in a medium saucepan and add the remaining ¼ cup wine. Cover and cook over medium-high heat, shaking pan often, until mussels open (about 5 minutes). Discard any that do not open.

5. Remove mussels from cooking liquid with a slotted spoon, reserving liquid, and transfer them to a deep serving dish. Cover mussels and keep them warm.

6. Put cleaned clams in a medium saucepan and add water. Cover and cook over medium-high heat, shaking pan often, until clams open (about 5 minutes). Discard any that do not open.

7. Remove clams from cooking liquid with a slotted spoon, reserving liquid, and transfer them to a deep serving dish. Cover clams and keep warm.

8. If cooking liquid of mussels or clams is sandy, leave it undisturbed for 10 minutes; then carefully pour it into a strainer lined with several layers of dampened cheesecloth and strain into another medium saucepan, leaving the sand behind.

9. Combine mussel and clam liquids. Gradually add half the shellfish liquid to the tomato mixture. Taste; if a saltier taste is desired, add more mussel and clam liquid.

10. Bring tomato mixture to a simmer. Reduce heat to low. Add shrimp, cover, and cook until shrimp are pink (about 2 minutes). Remove with slotted spoon.

11. Raise heat to medium-high and cook sauce until slightly thickened but not dry. Add parsley, tarragon, chives (if used), mussels and clams in their shells, and shrimp. Cover and heat briefly over low heat.

12. Stir in butter, 1 tablespoon at a time. Taste and add more pepper, if needed; salt will probably not be needed because mussels and clams are naturally salty. Serve in bowls.

Serves 4.

LAMB CURRY WITH GINGER AND COCONUT MILK

This curry, though fragrant with spices, is not very hot. If you prefer a fiery curry, increase the number of hot peppers or add some cayenne pepper or bottled hot-pepper sauce at the end. Wear gloves when handling the hot pepper in case your skin is sensitive to it. The unsweetened coconut required for the coconut milk can be purchased at health food stores. Serve the stew with rice and a green vegetable, such as peas or broccoli.

> 2 pounds lamb shoulder
> 3 tablespoons salad oil
> 2 medium onions, chopped
> 1 hot pepper (such as jalapeño), cored and minced
> 2 large cloves garlic, chopped
> 2 tablespoons chopped cilantro
> 2 tablespoons peeled, chopped fresh ginger
> Salt and pepper
> ¾ teaspoon turmeric
> 2 teaspoons ground cumin
> 2 teaspoons ground coriander seed
> 1 cup water
> Cilantro sprigs, for garnish (optional)

Coconut Milk

> 1 cup hot water
> 1 cup dried unsweetened coconut

1. Trim excess fat from lamb and cut meat into 1½-inch cubes.

2. Heat oil in a heavy casserole over medium-high heat. Add enough lamb cubes to make one layer and brown them. Remove to a plate with a slotted spoon; repeat with remaining cubes.

3. Reduce heat to medium-low, stir in onions, and cook until lightly browned (about 7 minutes). Stir in hot pepper, garlic, cilantro, and ginger; cook 30 seconds.

4. Return meat to pan and add any juices from plate. Add salt, pepper, turmeric, cumin, and coriander seed. Add the water and stir well. Bring to a boil. Reduce heat to low, cover, and simmer until meat is tender (about 1¾ hours).

5. Prepare Coconut Milk.

6. Skim excess fat from cooking liquid. Stir in Coconut Milk and cook, uncovered, over medium heat, stirring occasionally, until sauce thickens (about 10 minutes). Stew can be kept, covered, up to 3 days in refrigerator; reheat in uncovered casserole over low heat, stirring often.

7. Garnish stew with cilantro sprigs, if desired. Serve hot.

Serves 4.

Coconut Milk Combine the water and coconut in food processor or blender. Process for 30 seconds. Strain, pressing hard to extract as much liquid as possible; discard coconut.

VEAL WITH ARTICHOKES, PEAS, AND SAFFRON

Lighter in color and in texture than other meat stews, veal stews also cook faster. For an even quicker dish, you can use frozen artichoke hearts and peas instead of preparing fresh ones.

> Large pinch of saffron threads (about ⅛ tsp)
> About 2¼ cups water
> 1 tablespoon salad oil
> 3 tablespoons butter
> 2 pounds boneless veal shoulder or veal stew meat, cut in 1½-inch cubes
> 3 medium cloves garlic, chopped
> ¼ teaspoon salt
> ¼ teaspoon freshly ground pepper
> ¾ teaspoon ground ginger
> 1 lemon, halved
> 3 medium artichokes
> 1½ pounds fresh peas, shelled (about 1½ cups) and rinsed
> 1 to 2 tablespoons chopped fresh basil (optional)

1. Crush saffron between your fingers. Add to ¼ cup hot water and allow to soften for 20 minutes.

2. Heat oil and 1 tablespoon of the butter in a heavy casserole over medium-high heat. Add enough veal cubes to make one layer and brown them. Remove to a plate with a slotted spoon and repeat with remaining veal cubes.

3. Reduce heat to low. Add garlic and cook 30 seconds. Add saffron liquid to casserole and bring to a boil, stirring to dissolve any brown bits in casserole.

4. Return veal to pan and add any juices from plate. Sprinkle with salt, pepper, and ginger and stir over low heat to coat the meat with the spices. Pour in the remaining 2 cups water. Bring to a boil, skimming off froth that rises to top. Reduce heat to low, cover, and simmer, stirring occasionally, until veal is just tender when pierced with a knife (about 1 hour and 15 minutes).

5. Meanwhile, prepare artichoke bottoms: Squeeze juice of lemon half into a bowl of cold water; do not discard squeezed lemon. Break or cut off the stem of an artichoke. Break off largest leaves at bottom. Put artichoke on its side on a cutting board. Holding a very sharp knife or a serrated knife against side of artichoke, cut lower circle of leaves off, up to edge of artichoke bottom. Turn artichoke slightly after each cut. Rub edge of artichoke bottom well with cut lemon. Cut off central core of leaves just above artichoke bottom. Cut off leaves under base and trim base so it is round. Rub again with lemon. Put artichoke in bowl of lemon water. Continue with remaining artichokes.

6. Cut each artichoke in 4 pieces. Using a teaspoon, scoop out the hairlike "choke" from center of each piece. Return to water until ready to cook.

7. When veal is tender, remove it to a bowl with a slotted spoon. Spoon about 1 cup of cooking liquid into a medium saucepan. Add artichoke pieces. If necessary, add enough hot water to barely cover them. Cover and cook over low heat for 10 minutes. Uncover and continue to simmer until tender (about 15 minutes).

8. Pour remaining veal cooking liquid into another saucepan. Add peas and bring to a boil. Reduce heat to medium-low and simmer, uncovered, until just tender (about 10 minutes).

9. Return veal to casserole. When artichokes are tender, transfer them to casserole, using a slotted spoon. Boil artichoke cooking liquid until reduced to about ½ cup and add to casserole. Add peas and their cooking liquid. Simmer, uncovered, for 5 minutes. Stew can be kept, covered, up to 2 days in refrigerator; reheat in covered casserole over low heat.

10. Add the remaining butter to casserole and heat over low heat, shaking casserole gently, just until butter is absorbed. Add half the basil (if used). Taste and add more salt and pepper, if needed.

11. Serve the stew from the casserole or from a deep serving dish. Sprinkle with remaining basil (if used) just before serving.

Serves 4.

Light stews like Veal With Artichokes, Peas, and Saffron make use of spring vegetables to complement the meat. Serve the stew with white rice, noodles, or crusty French bread.

One of today's most popular cooking techniques, grilling is an excellent method for cooking meat and poultry, as well as firm fish (see page 113).

Roasting & Grilling

Few dishes can top the popularity of a roasted or grilled cut of meat, beautifully crusted on the outside and succulent inside. Roasting and grilling highlight the natural goodness of meat and fowl, giving us favorites such as roast leg of lamb (see page 100), roast beef (see page 104), and barbecued pork chops (see page 112). Behind these much-loved dishes lies the technique of cooking with dry heat. Its secrets are revealed in this chapter, which also includes step-by-step instructions for trussing poultry (see page 102) and carving (see page 105).

THE SECRETS OF ROASTING AND GRILLING

A great variety of meats and poultry can be roasted or grilled successfully, but they must be of good quality. The tenderest cuts of beef, veal, lamb, and pork produce the most delicious roasts and grilled meats. Generally, the same cuts of meat are suitable for both roasting and grilling; only the size of the cut determines which method is better. Roasting dries out a small piece of meat because the heat is less direct and the cooking takes longer, whereas the searing heat of the grill burns a large cut before it has had a chance to cook through.

To prevent lean meats from drying out and to add extra flavor before grilling or roasting, marinate them beforehand. The marinade is a seasoned liquid that is poured over the meat, which is then left to stand briefly at room temperature or refrigerated for a day or two so that the marinade can permeate it. Acids in the marinade, such as lemon juice or wine, tenderize the meat as well. The character of marinades can range from delicate, like the oil and lime juice marinade in Chicken Breasts With Chive Butter (see page 111), to spicy, like the yogurt-based marinade used for Spicy Roast Cornish Hens (see page 99).

To keep lean cuts of meat and poultry moist, baste them with their roasting juices, oil, melted butter, or a marinade during roasting or grilling. These liquids can be sprinkled, spooned, or brushed over the food.

The richest of roasted and grilled meats are moist enough to be served without sauce, although all roasted or grilled meats are enhanced by a sauce, especially a brown one such as Tomato-Mushroom Sauce With Tarragon (see page 41). Roasts are often served with a simple deglazing sauce made with the pan juices (see page 75). Flavored butters (see page 110) also add a festive accent to grilled meats.

For a complete main course, all sorts of vegetables can accompany roasted or grilled meats, from a simply cooked single vegetable to elaborate mixtures of seasonal vegetables, as in Roast Beef With Spring Vegetables (see page 104). Even fresh fruit can be used and is especially popular with poultry, as in Duck With Madeira and Pears (see page 106).

ROASTING

Large roasts are convenient holiday fare because one piece of meat, quite easily prepared, can serve many people. Served on a beautiful platter, a large roast surrounded by colorful vegetables always makes an impressive main course.

Roasting is ideal for the most tender cuts of meat. Not all cuts that are labeled "roast" at the store, however, are truly suitable for roasting. For beef, lamb, and pork, the rib roast is the most popular cut for roasting; it is sometimes called a "rack." In the case of pork and lamb, this type of roast is sometimes tied by the butcher into a crown roast. Another popular cut for roasting is the loin, especially of pork and veal. Leg of lamb, veal, or pork also make excellent roasts. Roasts should be relatively large so that they remain succulent. All types of poultry can be roasted, from Cornish hens to chickens, ducks, and turkeys.

Most meats, especially beef and lamb, are first seared at a high temperature to seal in the juices. For most cuts, the heat is then reduced so that they can continue roasting more slowly. Veal, pork, and poultry can be roasted by this method, or they can be roasted instead at a constant, lower temperature.

Before carving, the meat is left to rest for about 15 minutes on a board or platter in a warm place. All meats benefit from this resting period, but it is especially important for red meats. During this time, the meat juices, which were driven toward the center of the roast during cooking, are reabsorbed more evenly and the color of the meat becomes more uniform. In addition, less juice is lost during carving if the meat is left to stand. This resting period is very convenient for the cook, who can prepare gravy and finish cooking any vegetables during this time.

EQUIPMENT

Meat is roasted uncovered on a rack in a shallow roasting pan. The rack permits the heat to circulate all around the meat. If a rack is not available, however, the meat or poultry can be roasted directly in the pan. In fact, veal and pork, which are relatively dry meats, benefit from being in contact with the juices. The meat is roasted uncovered so that it will be cooked by dry heat rather than by the steam that would form under a cover.

It is best to use a heavy roasting pan so that the juices do not burn in the oven. The pan should be large enough so that no part of the meat extends beyond its edge; otherwise, some meat juices will drip into the oven. If the pan is much too large, however, the juices will burn. To roast a small bird or a relatively small cut of meat, you can use a heavy, shallow baking dish instead of a roasting pan.

A meat thermometer is the most reliable way to check whether a roast is done. The thermometer eliminates the guesswork that was once a part of roasting and gave rise to the famous saying of the French gastronome, Brillat-Savarin, "Cooks are made, roasters are born"—fortunately, no longer a true statement.

A bulb baster simplifies the job of basting with the pan juices because there is no need to tip a heavy pan to collect the juices with a spoon. A carving board with ridges to catch the juices is more convenient to use than a flat board. Poultry shears facilitate carving poultry.

SERVING

A traditional accompaniment to roasts is stuffing. A great variety of stuffings exist, but the most popular ones are based on bread, rice, or ground meat. The stuffing absorbs juices and flavor from the roast as it cooks and stretches the number of portions you get from expensive cuts of meat.

Gravy is a sauce served with roast meat, usually made from the pan juices. The technique for making gravy is very similar to that of making sauces by deglazing pans after sautéing meats (see page 75). To enhance the flavor of the pan juices, some cooks roast onions and carrots in the pan, as in Roast Beef With Spring Vegetables (see page 104).

A roast is beautiful served whole, but is easiest to carve in the kitchen. One way to have the best of both worlds is to present the whole roast on a platter, then take it back to the kitchen for carving. You can then arrange the pieces on the platter with the vegetables.

After 15 minutes of standing, roast meats can be kept warm for about 30 minutes longer in a low oven. Leftover roast meats can be cut in thin slices or cubes and reheated quickly in a frying pan with a little butter, some of the roasting juices, or some gravy or brown sauce. They are also delicious cut in thin slices and served cold, accompanied by a green salad.

SPICY ROAST CORNISH HENS

These Cornish hens stand in a spicy, yogurt-based marinade and turn reddish-brown when roasted. To carve a Cornish hen easily into two portions, cut it in half using poultry shears, cutting through the breast, then along the backbone. If desired, cut out the backbone before serving.

 1 *clove garlic, peeled*
 1 *tablespoon coarsely chopped peeled fresh ginger*
 ⅓ *cup plain yogurt*
 2½ *teaspoons paprika*
 1½ *teaspoons ground cumin*
 ½ *teaspoon turmeric*
 ¼ *teaspoon each cayenne pepper and ground cinnamon*
   Pinch each of freshly grated nutmeg and ground cloves
 ½ *teaspoon salt*
 2 *Cornish hens (about 1¼ lbs each)*

1. Combine garlic and ginger in food processor fitted with metal blade. Process until finely chopped. Add yogurt, paprika, cumin, turmeric, cayenne, cinnamon, nutmeg, cloves, and salt. Process until combined. (If a food processor is not available, chop garlic and ginger until very fine with a knife and mix with the remaining ingredients listed above.)

2. Place hens in a large bowl. Add yogurt mixture and rub it all over hens, inside and out. Cover and refrigerate for 1 day, turning occasionally.

3. Preheat oven to 400° F. Set hens on a rack in a roasting pan and spoon marinade over them. Roast until juices run clear when a skewer is inserted into thickest part of leg (about 50 minutes). If juices are pink, continue roasting a few more minutes. Let stand 5 minutes before serving.

Serves 2 to 4.

. . . ON ROASTING

□ *In choosing poultry for roasting, select a bird with its skin intact. The skin protects the meat, preventing it from drying.*

□ *If you are using frozen poultry, allow enough time to thaw the bird before roasting. Thawing a frozen duck in the refrigerator requires at least 24 hours and sometimes longer. A large frozen turkey may take up to three days to thaw.*

□ *Before cooking, allow the roast to come to room temperature, to facilitate quick and even cooking.*

□ *Skim excess fat from roasting juices before adding liquid to make sauce. (Tip the roasting pan and use a bulb baster or spoon to remove the fat.) Leave some fat, if desired, to add flavor.*

□ *Do not try to reheat a whole leftover roast, whether poultry or meat; the heat will take too long to reach the interior and the meat will dry out. Instead, remove the meat from the bones, cut it in small pieces, and heat it briefly in butter or sauce in a frying pan.*

CHECKING ROASTS WITH A MEAT THERMOMETER

You can check the internal temperature of a roast (either meat or poultry) with a meat thermometer, which is the simplest and most accurate indicator of its doneness, no matter what oven temperature you used to cook the roast. The thermometer should be inserted into the center of the thickest part of the roast and not in stuffing, fat, or bone.

If you use a standard meat thermometer, insert it after approximately three quarters of the cooking time has elapsed. A rapid-response or instant-reading thermometer is inserted for about 10 seconds, read, and removed. Most thermometers should be inserted at least 2 inches into the meat to get an accurate reading. For this reason, they are not used for small birds.

RECOMMENDED INTERNAL TEMPERATURES FOR ROASTS

Roast	Temperature
Beef	Rare: 135° F
	Medium-rare: 140° F
	Medium: 155° F
	Well-done: 170° F
Lamb	Rare: 135° F
	Medium-rare: 145° F
	Medium: 150° F
	Well-done: 160° F
Veal	160° F
Pork	165° F
Turkey	180° F

Note Beef and lamb can be roasted to taste, but veal, pork, and turkey should roast until they reach the internal temperatures given above.

LEG OF LAMB WITH GARLIC, POTATOES, AND ONIONS

Roasting juices from the lamb flavor the potatoes as they bake. Garlic slivers are inserted into the lamb to flavor the meat, and additional chopped garlic gives zest to the potatoes. Use a heavy roasting pan to prevent the vegetables from burning. Accompany this dish with green beans cooked until crisp-tender.

> 1 *leg of lamb (6 lbs)*
> 4 *medium cloves garlic, peeled*
> 6 *tablespoons butter, softened*
> ½ *teaspoon dried thyme*
> *Salt and pepper*
> 2½ *pounds large, all-purpose white potatoes*
> 2 *tablespoons salad oil*
> 2 *large onions, thinly sliced*

1. Preheat oven to 450° F. Trim skin from lamb and remove as much excess fat as possible.

2. Cut 2 of the garlic cloves in thin slices lengthwise, then in thin slivers. Make slits in lamb about 1 inch deep with a small, sharp knife, spacing them fairly evenly. Insert garlic slivers in slits.

3. Chop the remaining 2 cloves garlic with any remaining garlic slivers. Mix with butter, thyme, and salt and pepper to taste. Let stand at room temperature.

4. Peel potatoes, halve them lengthwise, and cut each half in crosswise slices about ¼ inch thick.

5. Set lamb on a rack in a large, heavy roasting pan. Spoon oil over lamb and sprinkle with salt and pepper. Roast for 15 minutes. Reduce oven to 350° F and roast, basting lamb occasionally with juices, for 20 minutes.

6. Remove lamb and rack from pan. Put potato and onion slices in lamb juices in pan and mix well. Sprinkle with salt and pepper. Scatter garlic and butter mixture over potatoes. Replace lamb on rack in pan over vegetables.

7. Continue roasting, stirring vegetables occasionally, until lamb is done to taste (about 1 hour). To check, insert a meat thermometer into thickest part of lamb; lamb is rare at 135° F, medium-rare at 145° F, medium at 150° F, and well-done at 160° F.

8. Transfer lamb to a carving board, cover loosely with foil, and let stand for 10 minutes. Taste a relatively thick potato slice; if it is not tender, continue baking vegetables for a few minutes. Taste vegetables and add more salt and pepper, if needed.

9. To carve lamb, hold shank bone with a towel and carve meat from rounded side of leg in several thin slices, cutting away from you. There is no need to carve all the way to the bone. Turn lamb over, carved side down, and cut meat from opposite side of leg. Last, carve slices from shank portion of meat, closest to the bone. Drain carving juices into a small saucepan and heat gently.

10. To serve, arrange lamb slices on a platter. Using a slotted spoon, transfer potato slices to platter or to separate serving dish. Pour juices remaining in roasting pan (which are mainly melted butter) into a small serving dish and heated carving juices into another.

Serves 10.

TURKEY WITH PECAN, MUSHROOM, AND ZUCCHINI STUFFING

The main problem in roasting turkey is keeping the breast meat moist in the long cooking time required. To prevent dryness, baste often with butter and cover the breast with foil for part of the roasting time. Traditional stuffing is bread flavored with fresh and dried herbs, vegetables, and nuts.

    1 turkey (14 lbs)
      Salt and pepper
    ¾ cup butter, softened
    ½ cup dry white wine
    3 cups Chicken Stock (see
      page 20)
    ¼ cup each butter and flour

Pecan, Mushroom, and Zucchini Stuffing

    1½ cups pecans
    ¾ cup butter
    ½ pound mushrooms, halved
      and cut in thin slices
      Salt and pepper
    2 large onions, chopped
    1 cup chopped celery
    3 cloves garlic, chopped
    ¾ pound zucchini, coarsely
      grated
    ½ pound day-old French or
      Italian bread, cut in ½-inch
      cubes (about 5 cups)
    ¼ cup each chopped parsley
      and chopped cilantro
    1½ teaspoons dried thyme

1. Prepare Pecan, Mushroom, and Zucchini Stuffing. Preheat oven to 400° F. Sprinkle turkey inside and out with salt and pepper. Spoon some stuffing into neck cavity. Fold neck skin under body and fasten with a skewer. Pack body cavity loosely with some stuffing and cover opening with a crumbled piece of foil. Truss turkey (see page 102). Spoon remaining stuffing into a buttered 4- to 6-cup baking dish.

2. Spread ½ cup of the butter over the skin. Put turkey in a large, oiled roasting pan, breast side up. Roast for 30 minutes.

3. Reduce oven to 325° F. Melt remaining ¼ cup butter. Roast turkey for 30 minutes, basting with melted butter every 15 minutes.

4. Cover turkey loosely with foil. Roast for 1 hour, basting turkey with any remaining melted butter and with pan juices every 30 minutes. If pan becomes dry, add ¼ cup of the wine. Put dish of extra stuffing in the oven.

5. Uncover turkey and continue roasting, basting every 15 minutes, until juices run clear when leg is pricked, or until meat thermometer inserted into thickest part of thigh registers 180° F (about 1¼ hours).

6. Transfer turkey carefully to platter or large board, discard strings and skewers, baste once with pan juices, and cover turkey.

7. Skim excess fat from juices in pan. Add the remaining wine and ½ cup of the stock to pan and bring to a boil, stirring and scraping to dissolve any brown bits in the pan. Boil until liquid is reduced to about ½ cup and strain into a bowl.

8. In a large, heavy saucepan over low heat, melt the ¼ cup butter. Whisk in flour. Cook, whisking constantly, until mixture turns a light beige color (about 3 minutes). Remove from heat and let cool slightly.

9. Gradually pour the remaining 2½ cups stock into flour mixture, whisking. Bring to a boil over medium-high heat, whisking constantly. Whisk in strained pan juices. Reduce heat to medium-low and simmer, uncovered, whisking often, until gravy is thick enough to coat a spoon (about 5 minutes). Taste and add salt and pepper, if needed.

10. Carve turkey and arrange on platter. Spoon stuffing onto platter or into a serving dish.

11. Reheat gravy briefly. Pour into a sauceboat and serve alongside turkey.

Serves 8 to 10.

Pecan, Mushroom, and Zucchini Stuffing

1. Preheat oven to 400° F. Put pecans in a baking dish and toast in oven for 7 minutes. Transfer to a bowl and let cool. Chop pecans coarsely.

2. In a large frying pan over medium-high heat, melt 2 tablespoons of the butter. Add mushrooms; add salt and pepper to taste and sauté until lightly browned (about 3 minutes). Transfer to a bowl.

3. In a very large frying pan over low heat, melt the remaining 10 tablespoons butter. Add onions and celery and cook, stirring, until softened (about 7 minutes). Add garlic and cook 30 seconds. Remove from heat.

4. Put grated zucchini into a colander and squeeze zucchini to remove excess liquid. Stir zucchini into onion mixture.

5. In a large bowl combine bread cubes, onion mixture, mushrooms, pecans, parsley, cilantro, thyme, and a pinch each of salt and pepper. With two large spoons, toss until ingredients are mixed thoroughly and bread is moistened. Taste and add more salt and pepper, if needed.

TRUSSING POULTRY

Trussing poultry before roasting keeps it in a neat shape, protects the breast meat with the skin of the neck, and prevents the legs and the wings from drying out. The method given here is one of the best; another good method is shown in the photograph on the opposite page. However, in a pinch you can just tie one piece of string around the wings and another around the legs.

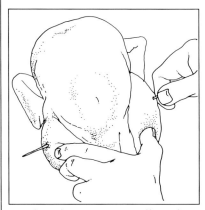

1. Thread a trussing needle with string and tie a knot at the needle's eye. Put the bird on its back and hold the legs pointing up. Insert the needle into one leg between the thigh and the drumstick.

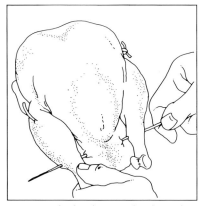

3. Turn the bird on its back and tie the ends of the string tightly. Rethread the needle and insert it through the lower part of the drumstick, then through the skin of the bird near the tail and through the end of the other drumstick.

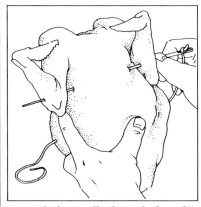

2. Push the needle through the sides of the bird below the breastbone and then out through the other leg. Turn the bird over. Push the needle through the closer wing, then under the backbone, then through the other wing, securing the wings to the back.

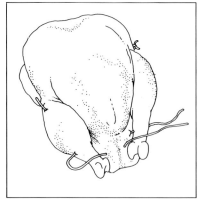

4. Bring string back through the skin near the tail. Tie the ends of the string tightly.

ROAST CHICKEN WITH RICE, FRUIT, AND ALMOND STUFFING

Although roasting chickens are slightly more flavorful than frying chickens, both can be roasted. The stuffing for this chicken is a variation of rice pilaf. If you like, serve the rice as a side dish with any roast, instead of as a stuffing. In this case, cook the rice for a total of 18 minutes.

½ cup slivered almonds
¼ cup salad oil
1 small onion, finely chopped
1 cup long-grain rice
1½ cups hot water
½ cup fresh, strained orange juice
Salt and pepper
1 small apple
½ cup raisins
¼ teaspoon ground cinnamon
1 roasting chicken (3½ to 4 lbs)

1. Preheat oven to 400° F. Toast almonds in a baking dish in oven, stirring occasionally, until lightly browned (about 5 minutes). Transfer to a bowl and let cool.

2. In a deep frying pan, heat 3 tablespoons of the oil over low heat. Add onion and cook, stirring often, until tender (about 5 minutes). Raise heat to medium, add rice, and sauté for 2 minutes. Add water, orange juice, salt, and pepper and bring to a boil. Reduce heat to low, cover, and cook for 10 minutes.

3. Meanwhile, peel, halve, and core apple and cut it in small dice. After rice has cooked 10 minutes, add apple and raisins to rice and stir very lightly with a fork. Cover and cook for 5 minutes; rice will be nearly tender. Stir in cinnamon and almonds. Taste and add more salt and pepper, if needed.

4. Sprinkle chicken with salt and pepper on all sides. Spoon enough rice stuffing into chicken to fill it, but do not pack it too tightly; reserve extra stuffing at room temperature.

5. Set chicken on a rack in a roasting pan and roast until juices run clear when a skewer is inserted into thickest part of leg (about 1 hour). If juices are pink, continue roasting chicken a few more minutes. Transfer chicken to a carving board. Let stand 5 to 10 minutes before serving.

6. Heat the remaining 1 tablespoon oil in a frying pan over low heat. Add remaining stuffing and cook, stirring often with a fork, until rice is tender and hot (about 3 minutes). Spoon into a serving dish.

7. Serve chicken and its stuffing on a platter. Serve remaining rice separately.

Serves 4.

Roasting at a fairly high temperature is the secret to tender, juicy chicken with crisp skin, as in Roast Chicken With Rice, Fruit, and Almond Stuffing.

Roast Beef With Spring Vegetables is a classic main course, the centerpiece of the most elegant of dinners, especially when made with a standing rib roast. The vegetables can be varied according to the season.

ROAST BEEF WITH SPRING VEGETABLES

Steamed New Potatoes With Parsley-Lemon Butter (see page 54) are a good accompaniment for the beef.

    1 *beef standing rib roast
       (5½ to 6 lbs), tied
       Salt and pepper*
    1 *large onion, quartered*
    1 *large carrot, cut in 4 chunks*
    ½ *pound thin carrots, cut in
       1½-inch chunks*
    ½ *pound baby onions, peeled*
    1½ *pounds green beans, ends
       removed, broken in 2 pieces*
    1 *medium cauliflower, divided
       into medium florets*
    ¼ *cup butter*

Gravy

    ⅓ *cup dry sherry*
    2 *cups Beef Stock (see
       page 21) or Brown Veal
       Stock (see page 21)*
    4 *teaspoons potato starch
       or arrowroot*
    2 *tablespoons water
       Salt and pepper (optional)*

1. Preheat oven to 500° F. Sprinkle beef evenly with salt and pepper. Set beef, bone side down, on a rack in a roasting pan and roast 15 minutes.

2. Carefully, to avoid splatters, add quartered onion and large carrot to pan. Reduce oven to 350° F and continue roasting, stirring onion and carrot occasionally, until a meat thermometer inserted in thickest part of beef registers 135° F for rare or 140° F for medium-rare (about 1¾ to 2 hours).

3. Put remaining carrots in a medium saucepan and add lightly salted water to cover. Bring to a boil, cover, and cook over medium heat until just tender (about 20 minutes). Drain; reserve at room temperature.

4. Put baby onions in a medium saucepan and add lightly salted water to cover. Bring to a boil, cover, and cook over medium heat until just tender (12 to 15 minutes). Drain thoroughly and reserve at room temperature.

5. In large saucepan boil enough lightly salted water to cover beans generously. Add beans; boil, uncovered, until just tender (about 8 minutes). Drain, rinse with cold water, drain again, and reserve at room temperature. Follow same process with cauliflower, boiling it about 7 minutes.

6. When roast is done, transfer it to a cutting board. Remove strings. Cover roast loosely with foil and let stand for 20 minutes.

7. Prepare Gravy.

8. Melt 2 tablespoons of the butter in each of two large frying pans over medium-low heat. Add carrots to one pan and cauliflower to second pan. Sprinkle vegetables with salt and pepper and sauté until hot. Remove and keep warm over very low heat. Put onions in one pan and green beans in the second. Sprinkle with salt and pepper and sauté until hot. Keep warm over very low heat while you carve the meat.

9. Carve about two thirds of roast into slices about ½ inch thick, and overlap the slices on a large serving platter. Also place uncarved portion of roast on platter. Surround meat with piles of vegetables. Transfer gravy to a sauceboat and serve separately.

Serves 8 to 10.

Gravy

1. Pour off fat from pan juices but leave onion and carrot in pan. Add sherry and ½ cup of the stock to pan and bring to a boil, stirring and scraping to dissolve any brown bits in the pan.

2. Strain into a medium saucepan, skim again to remove excess fat, and add the remaining 1½ cups stock. Bring to a boil.

3. Make a paste of potato starch and the water in a small cup. Add gradually to stock mixture, whisking. Simmer sauce, whisking, until thickened (about 3 minutes). Taste and add salt and pepper, if needed.

CARVING

When carving large cuts of meat or large birds, cut only enough slices for first servings, leaving the rest intact so that it will stay warm. If the roast becomes cold during carving, cover it and reheat it briefly on its platter in a hot oven.

Poultry

For any poultry, start by removing the leg and thigh from each side (see step 1 of "How to Cut Up Chicken for Stews," page 91). The cut-off pieces can then be divided into two sections or carved, according to their size.

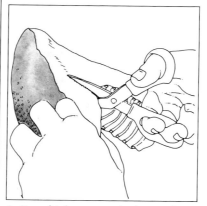

1. For chickens, *cut the breast from the back with poultry shears. Cut the breast section in half.*

2. For turkeys and ducks, *cut down the center of the breast section with a sharp knife. Cut under each breast half to separate it from the breast-bone. Remove the meat and slice it.*

Meats

Cuts of meat that have been boned, rolled, and tied can be simply sliced. The real challenge in carving meat is working around a bone. The process differs depending on the particular cut of meat. The leg of lamb illustrated here is representative of the technique of carving meat off a bone.

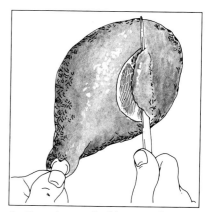

1. *Grasping end of bone with rounded side of leg toward knife, lift leg and tilt it away from the knife. Make the first cut parallel to the bone, cutting off just a thin slice.*

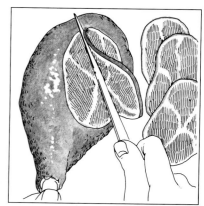

2. *Continue cutting meat in thin slices parallel to the bone. When you hit bone, turn the leg over and slice the other side in the same way.*

MARINATED ROAST VEAL WITH SPINACH AND PINE NUT STUFFING

For this dish, you'll need a roast that has been butterflied—cut almost in half and opened out flat so it can be stuffed and rolled. You can do this yourself, but it is easiest to ask the butcher to butterfly the meat and to pound it to the desired thickness. In the following recipe, the rolled roast is tied by a simple method. The sliced roast has a spiral of bright green spinach stuffing.

> 1 boned top round roast of veal (4¼ lbs), butterflied and pounded until about ¾ inch thick
> 2 teaspoons dried rosemary
> ½ cup olive oil
> ¼ cup dry white wine
> Salt and pepper
> ¼ cup butter, softened
> ⅓ cup Brown Veal Stock (see page 21), Beef Stock (see page 21), Chicken Stock (see page 20), or water
> 1½ cups Quick Brown Sauce (see page 40)

Spinach and Pine Nut Stuffing

> ½ cup pine nuts
> 4 cups water
> Salt
> ½ cup long-grain rice
> 1½ pounds spinach, leaves only, rinsed thoroughly
> 3 tablespoons olive oil
> 1 onion, finely chopped
> Pepper
> 4 large cloves garlic, minced
> 1 egg
> Pinch freshly grated nutmeg

1. Put roast in a deep dish and sprinkle it with rosemary on all sides. Pour olive oil and wine over meat. Cover and refrigerate, turning occasionally, for 2 hours or up to 1 day.

2. Prepare Spinach and Pine Nut Stuffing. Preheat oven to 375° F. Remove veal from dish, reserving olive oil marinade. Pat veal dry and open it on work surface. Sprinkle lightly with salt and pepper. Spread stuffing in smooth layer over veal, leaving a 1-inch border on all sides.

3. Beginning at a long edge, tightly roll meat into a cylinder. Tie a string around roast lengthwise, going around the sides of the cylinder. Tie another lengthwise string going from top to bottom. Tie additional lengths of string crosswise around the cylinder at 1½-inch intervals.

4. Set veal in a roasting pan. Rub with softened butter and sprinkle with salt and pepper. Roast for 15 minutes. Baste with about 2 tablespoons of reserved marinade. Reduce oven temperature to 325° F and continue roasting, basting every 15 minutes with marinade and with pan juices, until meat thermometer inserted in thickest part of meat registers 160° F (about 1 hour and 45 minutes).

5. Transfer veal to a carving board, cover loosely with foil, and let stand in a warm place about 15 minutes.

6. Pour off most of fat from pan juices. Add stock to pan. Bring to a boil, stirring and scraping to dissolve any brown bits in the pan. Strain into a bowl. Skim fat again, leaving a little to flavor sauce.

7. Bring Quick Brown Sauce to a boil. Whisk in strained pan juices. Taste and add salt and pepper, if needed. Pour into a sauceboat.

8. Using a sharp knife, cut veal into slices about ½ inch thick. Serve sauce separately.

Serves 8 to 10.

Spinach and Pine Nut Stuffing

1. Preheat oven to 400° F. Put pine nuts in a baking dish and toast in oven, stirring occasionally, until lightly browned (about 4 minutes). Transfer to a large bowl.

2. In a medium saucepan bring the water to a boil and add a pinch of salt. Add rice, stir once, and boil, uncovered, until tender (about 14 minutes); check by tasting. Drain, rinse with cold water, and leave to drain in strainer for 5 minutes.

3. In a large saucepan boil enough lightly salted water to cover spinach generously. Add spinach and cook, uncovered, over high heat, pushing leaves down into water often, until very tender (about 3 minutes). Rinse with cold water in colander and squeeze by handfuls until dry. Chop with a knife.

4. In a frying pan heat oil over medium heat. Add onion, salt, and pepper. Cook, stirring often, until onion is softened and begins to brown (about 7 minutes). Reduce heat to low, add garlic, and cook for a few seconds. Transfer to a bowl and let cool.

5. Add rice, spinach, onion mixture, egg, and nutmeg to bowl of pine nuts. Mix well. Taste and add more salt, pepper, and nutmeg, if needed.

DUCK WITH MADEIRA AND PEARS

For this simple but elegant dish, the pears are poached in spiced Madeira while the duck is roasting. The Madeira is then used to make a sauce for both duck and pears. Because ducks contain a lot of fat, their skin is pricked to allow the excess fat to escape during roasting.

> 1 duck (4½ lbs)
> Salt and pepper
> 1½ cups each Madeira and water
> 2 tablespoons sugar
> 2 whole cloves
> 4 ripe, firm pears
> ½ teaspoon fresh, strained lemon juice
> 1½ teaspoons potato starch, arrowroot, or cornstarch
> 1 tablespoon water

1. Preheat oven to 425° F. Remove any clumps of fat inside duck. If desired, truss duck (see page 102) to preserve its shape. Sprinkle duck with salt and pepper. Prick skin all over with a skewer.

106

2. Set duck on its side on a rack in a roasting pan. Roast it for 15 minutes. Spoon out excess fat from pan. Turn duck onto its other side. Roast duck 15 minutes longer. Reduce heat to 375° F. Set duck on its back and continue roasting, removing fat from pan as it collects and discarding it, until duck is done to taste (45 to 60 minutes). To test doneness, prick a thigh with a skewer: if juices run pink, duck is rare; if juices run clear, duck is well-done.

3. Meanwhile, prepare pears: Combine Madeira, water, sugar, and cloves in a medium saucepan. Bring to a boil, stirring. Remove from heat. Peel pears and halve them. Core them; then cut each piece in two lengthwise. Return Madeira mixture to a boil. Add pears, reduce heat to low, cover, and simmer until pears are tender when pierced with a knife (10 to 15 minutes). Discard cloves. Leave pears in their liquid.

4. When duck is tender, transfer it to a carving board, discard any trussing strings, and keep duck warm. Skim fat from roasting pan but leave layer of darker juices underneath.

5. Drain pears and add poaching liquid to roasting pan. Bring to a boil, stirring and scraping to dissolve any brown bits in the pan. Strain into a saucepan. Add lemon juice, taste, and add salt and pepper, if needed. Return to a simmer.

6. Stir the 1 tablespoon water into potato starch to get a smooth paste. Gradually whisk paste into simmering sauce. Return to just a simmer, add pears, and heat over low heat for 1 or 2 minutes.

7. Carve duck and set pieces on a platter. Garnish platter with pears. Spoon a little sauce over duck and pears. Serve remaining pears and sauce in a bowl.

Serves 2 or 3.

A classic technique combines with a contemporary stuffing in Marinated Roast Veal With Spinach and Pine Nut Stuffing. Serve it with Steamed New Potatoes With Parsley-Lemon Butter (see page 54) and with poached carrots.

... ON GRILLING
AND BROILING

☐ *In choosing poultry for grilling or broiling, select birds with the skin intact. The skin protects the meat, preventing it from drying.*

☐ *Bring the food to room temperature before grilling or broiling so that it cooks quickly and evenly.*

☐ *Never use a charcoal grill indoors or even partially indoors. Burning charcoal releases dangerous fumes, and the grill must be in the open air to allow adequate ventilation.*

☐ *Preheat the broiler with its rack and broiler pan inside for about 10 minutes before broiling food. A hot pan or grill is essential for searing the meat properly. If the grill is not hot enough, the meat will stick.*

☐ *For easier cleaning, line the broiler pan, but not the rack, with foil.*

☐ *Do not crowd the grill or broiler pan; crowding lowers the temperature of the pan and causes the meat to steam.*

☐ *Use tongs, not a fork, to turn the meat, because pricked meat loses its juices and becomes dry. When grilling, use long-handled tongs to avoid the heat of the coals.*

☐ *If the meat appears to be browning too fast and is in danger of scorching, move it to a part of the grill or broiler rack that is farther from the heat source. If meat browns unevenly, change the positions of the pieces.*

GRILLING AND BROILING

Grilling and broiling are very quick cooking methods that, until recently, were used mainly to prepare food for casual get-togethers and everyday meals. Now grilled foods have found their place on the menus of the best restaurants.

Grilling and broiling are similar methods and they achieve somewhat similar results. The meat or fish is seared by very high heat. In both grilling and broiling, the meat should be set on a rack, not in a pan, so that it will not stew in its juices. As in sautéing, the point is to cook the food through in the time it takes to brown the outside. Therefore, relatively small cuts are best.

Grilling is done over the heat on an outdoor grill or barbecue, while broiling takes place under the heat in an oven broiler. Grilling differs from broiling in that it gives the food a smoky flavor that many people enjoy. A number of fuels can be used; mesquite has become especially popular recently.

Indoors, you can grill on a ridged stovetop grill pan. The ridges elevate the meat, allowing it to cook in dry heat rather than boiling in its juices. In addition, the ridges mark the meat with an attractive line pattern. Grill pans with a nonstick surface are easiest to use.

Like roasting, grilling is most suited to tender cuts of meat. Rich meats are better than lean meats because their fat content helps prevent their drying out. The food most associated with grilling is a thick, juicy steak. Remember, however, that the word *steak*, like the word *roast*, is sometimes misapplied; not all cuts labeled "steak" are actually tender enough for broiling or grilling. The best ones to use are porterhouse, T-bone, club, rib-eye, or tenderloin steaks about 1½ inches thick. (Other "steaks," mainly from the chuck or round portion of the beef, are better for braising.) Chops—lamb, veal, or pork—are also good broiled or grilled. With chicken, pieces are more suitable for grilling than whole birds. Relatively thick fish fillets (about 1 inch thick) are also suitable, but thin, fragile fillets fall apart if broiled or grilled.

Grilled or broiled meats are served as soon as they are done. Serve sauces that accompany grilled meats separately to show off the appetizingly browned crust of the meat. As an alternative to a sauce, a simple flavored butter can be prepared (see page 110); in this case, a small dab of the butter is spooned onto the meat at serving time.

Almost any vegetable, rice, or pasta dish is a good complement to grilled or broiled meat. For a very quick meal, the meat can be accompanied instead by a green salad and fresh bread.

HOW TO PREPARE A CHARCOAL GRILL

A charcoal grill should be prepared at least 30 minutes before cooking begins. Mound the charcoal in the grill. To ignite it, you can saturate the coals with lighter fluid, or you can use an electric starter, which has the advantage of being odorless, but must be used with care. Allow the coals to burn until they are covered with white ash and then spread them out in an even layer.

About five minutes before the food is to be grilled, brush the rack lightly with oil, set it in place, and heat it. For most foods, the rack should be about 4 to 6 inches above the coals.

LAMB CHOPS WITH FRESH PEPPER AND TOMATO SAUCE

Grilled lamb chops are rich enough to be served without accompaniment, but for a special treat, serve them with a spicy sauce, such as this one.

> 1 fresh jalapeño pepper
> 3 tablespoons salad oil
> 1 large onion, chopped
> 2 red bell peppers, chopped
> 2 cloves garlic, chopped
> 1½ pounds ripe tomatoes, peeled, seeded, and chopped
>   Salt and pepper
> 8 rib lamb chops, about 1½ inches thick

1. Discard seeds and ribs from jalapeño; chop pepper finely. Immediately wash your hands, cutting board, and knife.

2. In a deep frying pan over low heat, heat 2 tablespoons of the oil. Add onions; cook, stirring often, until soft but not browned (about 5 minutes). Add bell peppers, garlic, and jalapeño; cook, stirring often, until peppers soften (about 5 minutes).

3. Add tomatoes and a pinch of salt and raise heat to medium. Cook, uncovered, stirring often, until mixture is thick (about 30 minutes). Taste and add more salt, if needed. The sauce can be refrigerated, covered, for about 4 days, or frozen.

4. Prepare grill or preheat broiler with rack about 3 inches from heat source.

5. Trim excess fat from chops, brush both sides with the remaining tablespoon of oil, and sprinkle them with salt and pepper. Put chops on hot grill or hot broiler rack; grill or broil until done (about 6 minutes per side for medium-rare). To check for doneness, press meat with your finger. Rare lamb does not resist; medium-rare lamb resists slightly; well-done lamb is firm.

6. Meanwhile, reheat sauce in a saucepan over medium heat. Transfer chops to platter. Serve sauce separately.

Serves 4.

A hearty sauce with plenty of flavor, like Fresh Pepper and Tomato Sauce, is the best accent for grilled lamb chops. Serve them with French-Fried Potatoes (see page 81), steamed potatoes, or crusty French or Italian bread.

FLAVORED BUTTERS

Flavored butters are an excellent accompaniment for grilled meats and fish. Lighter than sauces, they particularly appeal to those who prefer to avoid rich foods. Examples of this style of topping food are Steaks With Roquefort Butter and Chicken Breasts With Chive Butter, both at right.

Herb butters are made of softened butter mixed with salt, pepper, and any fresh herb in season—parsley, dill, tarragon, cilantro, or chives, for instance. Dried herbs can be used if fresh herbs are not available, but the fresh ones are preferable. Citrus juice, garlic, and spices can also be used in flavored butters. Flavored butter can be refrigerated, covered, for a week, or frozen.

To serve, bring the butter to room temperature and, at the last minute, spoon it onto the meat or fish when it is already on the plates, so that the hot food begins to melt the butter into a "sauce." Herb butter can also be stirred gently into hot, well-drained pasta, rice, potatoes, or vegetables.

STEAK WITH RED WINE AND HERB SAUCE

In this recipe, a large steak is grilled whole and then sliced into portions. Instead of a porterhouse steak, a T-bone or club steak can be used.

- 1 cup dry red wine
- 1 shallot, chopped
- ¼ teaspoon each *dried thyme* and dried marjoram
- 1 cup Basic Brown Sauce (see page 39) or Quick Brown Sauce (see page 40)
- 1 porterhouse steak (about 1½ lbs), about 1½ inches thick
- 1 tablespoon salad oil Salt and pepper
- 2 tablespoons cold butter, cut in 2 pieces
- 2 teaspoons thinly sliced chives
- 1 tablespoon chopped parsley Pinch of sugar (optional)

1. Prepare grill or preheat broiler with rack about 4 inches from heat source.

2. In a medium saucepan bring wine to a boil with shallot, thyme, and marjoram. Boil, stirring occasionally, until wine is reduced to about ¼ cup.

3. Strain wine into medium saucepan, pressing on shallots. Whisk in brown sauce. Bring to a boil, whisking. Simmer until sauce is thick enough to coat a spoon.

4. Brush both sides of steak with oil. Sprinkle with salt and pepper. Put on hot broiler rack or grill. Broil or grill until browned on both sides and done to taste (about 6 minutes per side for medium-rare); rare steak does not resist when pressed, medium-rare steak resists slightly, medium-done steak resists slightly more, and well-done steak is springy to the touch.

5. Bring sauce to a boil. Remove from heat and stir in cold butter, chives, and parsley. Taste and add salt and pepper, if needed; if flavor is too tart, add a pinch of sugar.

6. To serve, cut steak in thin slices. Pour a little sauce over each portion. Serve remaining sauce separately.

Serves 4.

STEAKS WITH ROQUEFORT BUTTER

Serve these steaks with baked or steamed potatoes. Instead of the Roquefort Butter, Béarnaise Sauce (see page 44) or any brown sauce can accompany these steaks. Sirloin steaks can also be prepared in this way, but rib-eye steaks are more tender.

- 4 rib-eye steaks, about 1½ inches thick
- 1 tablespoon salad oil Pepper

Roquefort Butter

- 6 tablespoons unsalted butter, softened
- ¼ cup crumbled Roquefort cheese
- 2 teaspoons brandy
- 1 tablespoon chopped parsley Pepper

1. Preheat broiler with rack about 3 inches from heat source or prepare grill.

2. Brush steaks with oil on both sides and sprinkle with pepper. Put on hot broiler rack or grill. Broil or grill until browned on both sides and done to taste (about 5 minutes per side for medium-rare); rare meat does not resist when pressed, medium-rare meat resists slightly, medium-done meat resists slightly more, and well-done meat is springy to the touch.

3. Remove from heat and put a tablespoon of Roquefort Butter on each steak. Serve immediately. Serve remaining Roquefort Butter separately.

Serves 4.

Roquefort Butter Beat butter with Roquefort, brandy, and parsley. Add pepper to taste. Cover and refrigerate for 1 hour to blend flavors. Bring to room temperature before serving.

CHICKEN BREASTS WITH CHIVE BUTTER

You can keep chicken breasts moist during broiling or grilling by dotting them with butter and brushing them with marinade. Both techniques are used in this recipe. Chive Butter is also spooned onto the chicken at serving time to form a simple sauce.

¼ cup salad oil
2 tablespoons fresh, strained lime juice
  Pepper
  Half an onion, sliced
4 unskinned, boneless chicken breast halves (about 6 oz each)
  Salt
  Lime wedges, for garnish (optional)

Chive Butter

6 tablespoons butter, softened
1 teaspoon fresh, strained lime juice
2 tablespoons thinly sliced chives
  Salt and pepper

1. Prepare Chive Butter.

2. In a shallow dish mix oil, lime juice, pepper, and onion. Add chicken and turn until coated with mixture. Cover and marinate at room temperature 1 hour or in refrigerator up to 6 hours, turning from time to time.

3. Preheat broiler with rack about 4 inches from heat source, or prepare grill.

4. Remove chicken from marinade, removing any pieces of onion that cling to it. Discard onion, reserving remaining marinade. Set chicken breasts, skin side up, on plate and spoon 1 teaspoon Chive Butter onto each. Sprinkle chicken with salt and pepper.

5. Set chicken on broiler rack or grill, with skin side nearest heat source. Broil or grill, brushing once or twice with marinade, for 3 minutes.

6. Turn chicken over with tongs and quickly spoon another teaspoon Chive Butter onto center of each piece. Broil or grill, brushing once with marinade, until meat feels springy (about 3 minutes).

7. Remove from heat. Put a tablespoon of Chive Butter onto each chicken breast. Garnish plates with lime wedges, if desired. Serve immediately. Serve remaining Chive Butter separately.

Serves 4.

Chive Butter Beat butter with lime juice and chives. Season with salt and pepper to taste. Cover and refrigerate at least 2 hours to allow flavors to blend. Bring to room temperature before using.

A ridged stove-top grill pan is ideal for grilling chicken breasts, which should be cooked briefly so they do not dry out. For a quick meal, serve grilled Chicken Breasts With Chive Butter accompanied by blanched broccoli and toasted almonds.

Pork chops brushed with Easy Barbecue Sauce cook quickly on an outdoor grill or in an oven broiler. You might want to serve them with French-Fried Potatoes (see page 81) or buttered corn.

GRILLED PORK WITH EASY BARBECUE SAUCE

The bright red sauce used in this dish gives a slightly spicy, sweet-and-sour taste to meats. (You can also brush this sauce on chicken breasts before broiling.) Serve the pork with vegetables that stand up to the flavor of the sauce. Carrots, cauliflower, and potatoes are good choices.

> 3 tablespoons *salad oil*
> One fourth of a large or half a small *onion,* finely chopped
> ½ cup *catsup*
> 1 tablespoon each *brown sugar and red or white wine vinegar*
> 1 teaspoon *chili powder*
> 1 tablespoon *Dijon mustard*
> *Salt and pepper*
> 4 *pork chops,* about 1 inch thick

1. In a medium saucepan heat 2 tablespoons of the oil over low heat. Add onion and cook, stirring, until soft (about 7 minutes). Stir in catsup, brown sugar, vinegar, and chili powder and bring to a simmer. Remove from heat and stir in mustard. Taste and add salt and pepper, if needed. Cool to room temperature.

2. Prepare grill or preheat broiler with rack about 6 inches from heat source.

3. Trim excess fat from pork chops. Brush both sides of pork with the remaining 1 tablespoon oil and sprinkle with salt and pepper.

4. Put pork chops on hot grill or hot broiler rack. Cook chops until they are tender when pierced with a thin, sharp knife and meat juices run clear, not pink, when meat is pricked (about 10 minutes per side), quickly brushing them every few minutes with generous amounts of sauce. Serve hot.

Serves 4.

GRILLED FISH FILLETS WITH MINT BÉARNAISE SAUCE

A rich sauce is a perfect complement to grilled fish, but if you're in a hurry, prepare an herb butter instead (see page 110). Serve the fish with green vegetables and steamed potatoes or rice.

> 1½ pounds swordfish, shark, or halibut fillet, about 1 inch thick, rinsed and patted dry
> 2 teaspoons fresh, strained lemon juice
> 1 tablespoon salad oil
> Béarnaise Sauce (see page 44)
> 4 teaspoons chopped fresh mint
> Salt and pepper
> Fresh mint sprigs, for garnish

1. If you are using shark, trim off any dark red meat. Cut fish in 4 pieces and put them in shallow bowl. Sprinkle with lemon juice and oil. Let stand at room temperature for 30 minutes, turning twice.

2. Prepare grill, or preheat broiler with rack about 2 inches from heat source.

3. Prepare Béarnaise Sauce and add mint. Keep sauce warm in a pan set on a rack above a pan of hot water.

4. Sprinkle fish lightly with salt and pepper. Arrange on broiler pan or grill, in batches if necessary to avoid crowding. Broil or grill until fish are just opaque and tender, or until a skewer inserted into fish comes out hot to touch (about 3 minutes on each side).

5. Transfer fish to plates and garnish with mint sprigs. Serve sauce separately.

Serves 4.

CHICKEN LEGS BROILED WITH ORANGE AND SOY SAUCE

Chicken legs require slightly longer to broil than breasts but are richer and remain moist without the addition of butter. Serve this citrus-flavored chicken with rice and with cooked baby onions or carrots, or a simple green salad.

> ¼ cup each soy sauce and fresh, strained orange juice
> 2 tablespoons each fresh, strained lemon juice and salad oil
> 1 tablespoon honey
> 1 teaspoon grated orange rind
> 1 medium shallot, minced
> 1 teaspoon ground ginger
> ¼ teaspoon ground cloves
> Pinch of pepper
> 4 chicken legs, cut into drumsticks and thighs (about 2¾ lbs)
> 4 thin slices orange, for garnish (optional)

1. In a shallow dish mix soy sauce, orange juice, lemon juice, oil, honey, orange rind, shallot, ginger, cloves, and pepper. Add chicken pieces and turn them over in mixture. Rub mixture thoroughly into chicken. Cover and refrigerate chicken for 2 hours or up to 24 hours, turning occasionally.

2. Preheat broiler with rack about 6 inches from heat source, or prepare grill. Remove chicken from soy marinade. Reserve marinade and put chicken on hot broiler rack or grill. Broil or grill chicken, turning and brushing with marinade about every 2 minutes, for 7 minutes.

3. Move chicken so that it is farther from heat source and continue broiling or grilling, turning often and brushing often with soy marinade, until leg pieces are tender when pierced in thickest part with a thin, sharp knife and juices run clear, not pink (about 8 minutes).

4. Transfer to a platter or plates and garnish with orange slices, if desired. Serve hot.

Serves 4.

GRILLED SHRIMP WITH DILL SOUR CREAM

For this very simple dish, the shrimp are grilled in their shells to protect their delicate flesh from the heat. They can be served hot or cold and are ideal for either an appetizer or a buffet dish.

> ½ cup sour cream
> 4 teaspoons snipped fresh dill
> Salt and pepper
> 8 large shrimp (about 5 oz), unshelled, rinsed

1. Mix sour cream with dill and add salt and pepper to taste. Transfer to a bowl. Refrigerate 1 hour, if desired, to blend flavors. Bring to room temperature before serving.

2. Prepare grill, or preheat broiler with rack about 2 inches from heat source.

3. Slit the back of each shrimp with a very sharp, small knife (this will aid in shelling the hot shrimp after cooking). Grill or broil shrimp until shells turn bright pink (about 1½ minutes per side). Remove to plate. If desired, shell shrimp (see page 15) and scrape out the "vein" (do not place under running water).

4. Serve shrimp, either hot or at room temperature, on a platter. Serve sauce separately.

Serves 4 as an appetizer or 2 as a main dish.

113

One of the simplest desserts is best-quality fresh fruit topped with a rosette of whipped cream—a beautiful garnish, delicious and easy to do.

Dessert Techniques

Whether an elaborate tour de force or a simple sweet to end a meal, desserts are based on a relatively small number of cooking techniques. In this chapter you will find desserts of two types: fruit (such as Sautéed Bananas With Rum, page 118, and Crêpes With Apples and Calvados, page 119) and cream- or custard-based (such as Basic Chocolate Mousse and Lemon Soufflé, both on page 123). Eggs are an important ingredient in many desserts; you'll find "Tips on Working With Eggs" on page 121.

DESSERT TECHNIQUES

This chapter concentrates on basic techniques important to dessert-making. The recipes, chosen to illustrate these procedures, are divided into two categories: simple fruit desserts, in which fruit makes up the major part of the dessert, and creamy desserts, based on custards or cream. (For other dessert techniques, consult the California Culinary Academy cookbook *Cakes & Pastries*.)

Certain techniques already covered in previous chapters are also used in dessert-making, in particular poaching (see page 57) and sautéing (see page 70), which are used to cook many types of fruit. In addition, a number of procedures are specific to dessert-making, several of them involving the use of eggs. Egg yolks add richness to desserts, while egg whites add lightness. To prepare many desserts, such as Lemon Soufflé (see page 123) and Basic Chocolate Mousse (see page 123), you need to know how to whip egg whites properly and, once they are beaten, how to combine them with other ingredients so that they remain light and airy. See "Tips on Working With Eggs," page 121, for directions on preparing eggs.

Most desserts are made according to a relatively small number of basic patterns. Members of the dessert "families" differ from one another mainly in their flavorings—vanilla, coffee, chocolate, nuts, grated rinds, fruits, or liqueurs. Once you are familiar with the major techniques, you can apply them to a great variety of desserts.

A good, heavy-duty electric mixer with both a whip and a flat beater makes it easy to perform procedures such as beating egg whites, whipping cream, creaming butter, and the like. Somewhat less efficient but still effective is a hand-held electric mixer.

SIMPLE FRUIT DESSERTS

A number of very pleasing desserts can be made from raw or cooked fruit. Generally, very soft fruits, such as most berries, are used raw, and firm, crunchy fruits, such as apples, are cooked. Some fruits, like pineapple, can be used raw, poached, or sautéed.

These simple, quick-to-prepare fruit desserts make refreshing finales when served alone after a rich meal but become especially festive when accompanied by whipped cream, ice cream, or sorbet. They are often part of more complex desserts. Sautéed fruit, for example, makes a good filling for crêpes, as in Crêpes with Apples and Calvados (see page 119).

A particularly apt flavoring for fruit desserts is a liqueur or brandy that matches the fruit. If it is not practical to have all the fruit liqueurs on hand at any one time, you can make do with kirsch and orange-flavored liqueur, which are good all-around spirits that are delicious with most fruits. Among the stronger spirits, brandy and rum are the most useful.

SIMPLE DESSERT SAUCES

Use these sauces together with poached or raw fruit and with ice cream to create a variety of sundaes. For example, combine poached peaches or nectarines with raspberry sauce and vanilla ice cream; or serve poached pears with chocolate sauce and chocolate-chip ice cream.

RASPBERRY SAUCE

>   2   *cups fresh or thawed frozen raspberries*
>   4   *to 5 tablespoons confectioners' sugar, sifted (optional)*
>   1   *to 2 tablespoons kirsch (optional)*

Purée raspberries in a food processor or blender until very smooth. Strain into a bowl, pressing the purée through the mesh. If you are using fresh or unsweetened frozen berries, whisk in 4 tablespoons sugar. Taste and add more sugar, if needed. Add kirsch, if desired. Refrigerate until ready to use. Sauce can be kept, covered, up to 2 days in refrigerator.

Makes about 1 cup.

CHOCOLATE SAUCE

>   4   *ounces semisweet chocolate, chopped*
>   ⅓   *cup whipping cream*

Combine chocolate and cream in a small, heavy saucepan. Heat over very low heat until chocolate melts. Stir until sauce is smooth. For a thicker sauce, continue cooking until sauce thickens to taste. Sauce can be kept, covered, up to 1 week in refrigerator. Reheat in a saucepan set in a shallow pan of hot water before serving.

Makes about ½ cup.

FRUIT SALAD WITH LIQUEUR AND WHIPPED CREAM

Any fruit can be made into fruit salad, but the best are the soft fruits. Instead of or in addition to the fruits specified in this recipe, you can use oranges, tangerines, peaches, apricots, plums, blueberries, bananas, or grapes. It is best to have a colorful selection of fruits. You can use any fruit-flavored liqueur instead of orange to add excitement to the salad, or you can replace the liqueur with fresh orange juice or an additional tablespoon of lemon juice. A scoop of vanilla ice cream or fruit sorbet can top each serving in place of the whipped cream.

>   3 medium nectarines
>   1 pint strawberries, lightly
>   rinsed and hulled
>   1 pint blackberries or
>   raspberries
>   3 tablespoons sugar
>   2 teaspoons fresh, strained
>   lemon juice
>   2 tablespoons orange-
>   flavored liqueur

Whipped Cream

>   1 cup whipping cream
>   2 teaspoons sugar
>   1 teaspoon vanilla extract

1. Slice nectarines in wedges, cutting inward toward the pits. Put the slices in a bowl. Quarter strawberries lengthwise and add to bowl. Add blackberries.

2. Sprinkle fruit with sugar, lemon juice, and liqueur. Using a rubber spatula, mix ingredients as gently as possible. Taste and add more sugar, lemon juice, and liqueur, if needed. Cover with plastic wrap and chill for about 1 hour.

3. To serve, divide fruit mixture among 4 to 6 stemmed glasses or dessert dishes. Pipe a large rosette of whipped cream on top of each. Serve remaining cream separately.

Serves 4 to 6.

Whipped Cream Chill bowl and beater for whipping cream. With mixer at high speed, whip cream with sugar and vanilla in chilled bowl until stiff. Cream can be whipped up to 2 hours ahead and kept in refrigerator, but it retains its shape best when whipped a short time before serving. Spoon whipped cream into a pastry bag fitted with a medium star tip.

Light, colorful Fruit Salad With Liqueur and Whipped Cream is an excellent ending for a rich dinner.

USING A PASTRY BAG

With only a little practice and a pastry bag with tips, you can make beautiful dessert decorations. The most useful tip for decorating is a medium-sized star, sometimes called a zigzag or fluted tip. The technique is shown here with chocolate frosting on marble for best visibility.

1. To fill a pastry bag, first insert the tip. Fold the top of the bag back over one hand and hold the bag open. Using a rubber spatula, scoop up the mixture to be piped and put it in the bag. When the bag is filled, unfold the top to enclose the mixture and push the mixture downward toward the tip. Twist the top of the bag down to the mixture.

2. To pipe, hold the bag in one hand and let the tip end rest on the other hand. Holding the tip at least a half inch above the surface of the dessert, press with the hand that holds the bag to squeeze out the mixture; guide the tip with the other hand. The photo above shows four different designs you can make with a small open-star tip.

POACHED FRUIT IN SYRUP

Poached fruit is a wonderful accompaniment for vanilla or fruit-flavored ice cream, especially when served with sauces (see page 116), and is also a popular ingredient in fillings for crêpes, cakes, and pastries. The fruit is poached in a simple syrup of sugar and water flavored with lemon juice and vanilla. There should be enough syrup to cover the fruit so that it cooks evenly; if there is not enough syrup, it is best to cook the fruit in batches. Fruit should always be poached over very low heat so it does not fall apart. Left to cool in its syrup, the fruit absorbs flavor and remains moist. Almost any fruit can be poached, but those listed below are used most often.

> ¾ cup sugar
> 3 cups water
> Half a lemon (if using pears, you will need a whole lemon)
> 1 vanilla bean (optional)
> 1½ pounds pears, peaches, nectarines, or pineapple

1. Combine sugar, water, juice of half a lemon, and vanilla bean (if used) in a large, heavy saucepan. Heat over low heat, stirring gently, until sugar dissolves. Bring to a boil. Remove from heat.

2. If using pears, peel them with a vegetable peeler and rub them with the other half of the lemon, squeezing a little lemon juice on them, to prevent them from turning brown; halve pears and remove cores with tip of peeler. If using peaches or nectarines, halve or quarter them and remove pits. If using pineapple, cut off peel with a sharp knife and cut off brown "eyes"; cut pineapple in crosswise slices.

3. Return syrup to a boil. Add fruit and bring to a simmer. Reduce heat to low, cover with a lid slightly smaller in diameter than that of the saucepan to keep the fruit immersed, and cook until fruit is tender when pierced with a sharp knife (about 12 minutes for pears and about 8 minutes for peaches, nectarines, and pineapple).

4. Remove from heat and let fruit cool completely in syrup. If using peaches, pull off peel. Transfer fruit and syrup gently to a bowl or other container and chill. Fruit can be kept for 3 days in refrigerator. Serve cold or at room temperature. If serving fruit alone, serve in a bowl with a few spoons of the syrup.

Serves 4 to 6.

SAUTÉED BANANAS WITH RUM

Sautéing is an excellent technique for cooking firm fruit, especially apples, pears, pineapple, and bananas. Butter, not oil, is used, and the fruit acquires a wonderfully buttery flavor. Serve these bananas alone, with vanilla or chocolate ice cream, or with whipped cream.

> ¼ cup unsalted butter
> 4 ripe, relatively firm bananas, peeled and halved crosswise
> 2 tablespoons sugar
> 2 to 3 tablespoons rum

1. Heat butter in a large frying pan over medium heat. When butter is very hot, add bananas and sauté until they are golden on each side (about 3 minutes).

2. Raise heat to high and sprinkle bananas with sugar. Sauté, rolling bananas around, until sugar dissolves (about 30 seconds).

3. Add 2 tablespoons of the rum and bring to a boil. Taste and add more rum, if needed. Serve hot.

Serves 4.

CHERRIES IN RED WINE

For this dish, red wine is used to make a poaching syrup. After the fruit is poached, the syrup is made into a light sauce. This is a convenient way to prepare cherries because they do not require pitting. The stem is left on to show that the cherries contain their pits, but it is usually a good idea to warn people anyway! Pears, peaches, and nectarines are also good when poached in this way, but their cooking times are longer. They should be cut and peeled as for poaching in syrup (see Poached Fruit in Syrup, page 118).

> 1½ cups dry red wine
> 3 tablespoons sugar
> ¼ teaspoon ground cinnamon
> 1 pound sweet dark cherries
>   (about 2½ cups)
> 1 tablespoon red currant jelly
>   or other red jelly

1. Combine red wine, sugar, and cinnamon in a medium-sized, heavy saucepan. Heat over low heat, stirring gently, until sugar dissolves. Bring to a boil. Remove from heat.

2. For a more attractive presentation, cut off tips of cherry stems using scissors.

3. Bring syrup to a boil. Add cherries to syrup and bring to a simmer. Reduce heat to low, cover, and cook until tender (about 10 minutes). Remove from heat, uncover, and let cherries cool in wine for 30 minutes.

4. Drain wine into another saucepan. Boil wine over medium-high heat until it is reduced to about ½ cup. Reduce heat to low, add jelly, and cook, stirring, until jelly melts.

5. Carefully transfer cherries to a deep serving dish or a bowl. Pour wine sauce over cherries and let cool. Refrigerate until thoroughly chilled (about 2 hours). Cherries can be kept up to 3 days in refrigerator. Serve cold, in the sauce.

Serves 4.

CRÊPES WITH APPLES AND CALVADOS

Crêpes can be accompanied simply with unsalted butter, sugar, and jam, or they can be wrapped around a filling of sautéed fruit, as in this recipe. The apple filling also makes a good dessert on its own, top it with whipped cream or sour cream and a few chopped nuts. You can substitute brandy for the Calvados, or instead flavor the apples with lemon juice or cinnamon to taste.

> 5 to 6 tablespoons unsalted
>   butter
> ¾ cup flour, sifted
> ¾ cup milk
> ½ cup water
> 3 eggs
> ½ teaspoon salt
> 2 tablespoons salad oil
>   (for brushing pan)

Apple Filling

> 2 pounds Golden Delicious
>   apples
> ¼ cup unsalted butter
> 6 to 8 tablespoons sugar
> 4 to 6 tablespoons Calvados
>   (apple brandy)

1. In a small saucepan over low heat, melt 2 tablespoons of the butter; remove from heat and let cool.

2. Combine melted butter, flour, milk, water, eggs, and salt in a food processor fitted with metal blade or in a blender; blend for 5 seconds. Scrape down sides of container and blend for 20 seconds. Pour into a bowl, cover, and refrigerate 1 hour.

3. Heat a 7-inch crêpe pan or frying pan briefly over medium-high heat. Brush pan lightly with salad oil, heat again, and remove pan from heat. Stir batter. Half-fill a ¼-cup measure with batter and pour it into pan. Tilt and turn pan quickly so that batter covers bottom in a thin layer; pour any excess batter back in bowl. Return pan to heat, loosen edge of crêpe with a metal spatula, and cook until crêpe is lightly browned. Turn over and brown second side briefly. Transfer crêpe to a plate.

4. Make crêpes with remaining batter in the same manner, brushing pan lightly with oil as necessary. Pile crêpes on plate and keep them warm. The crêpes can be kept, wrapped in plastic wrap, up to 1 day in refrigerator or they can be frozen. Bring crêpes to room temperature before continuing.

5. Preheat oven to 450° F. Butter 2 shallow baking dishes.

6. Spoon 1 to 2 tablespoons filling onto the less attractive side of each crêpe near one edge and roll them like cigars. Arrange in one layer in baking dishes. Cut remaining 3 to 4 tablespoons butter in small pieces and dot the crêpes with cut butter.

7. Bake until very hot (about 5 minutes). Serve from the baking dishes.

Serves 8.

Apple Filling

1. Peel and halve apples. Core them using the point of the peeler and cut them in thin wedges or slices.

2. Divide butter between 2 large frying pans and melt it over medium-high heat. Add apples to pans and sauté, turning the pieces over from time to time, until they are coated with butter. Cover, reduce heat to low, and cook until apples are just tender (about 10 minutes).

3. Raise heat to high and add 3 tablespoons sugar to each pan, turning apple wedges over so both sides are coated with sugar. Leave pans over high heat just until sugar dissolves.

4. Combine apples in one of the frying pans. Reduce heat to low. Add 4 tablespoons Calvados and heat briefly. Remove from heat. Taste and add more sugar, if needed; heat, tossing apples gently, just until sugar dissolves. Taste again and add more Calvados, if desired. Filling can be made 1 day ahead without Calvados and kept in refrigerator; reheat before filling crêpes and add Calvados.

By combining fruit purée with whipped cream, a simple syrup, and a little gelatin, you can make a smooth and velvety fruit dessert like this Strawberry Mousse.

CREAMY DESSERTS

This category includes many favorite dessert types—such as mousses, souf-flés, and custards—that are both rich and light. Their popularity stems from their smooth, delicate texture. Some are cooked, some are baked, and others require no cooking at all.

The creamy texture of these desserts is due either to a generous quantity of whipped cream, as in Strawberry Mousse (at right), or to a custard of eggs, milk, and sugar, as in Baked Chocolate Custard (see page 122). Soufflés are made of a custard-like base lightened with egg whites.

To succeed in preparing these desserts, you need to pay particular attention to beating the cream and egg whites properly (see "Tips on Working With Eggs," at right). The special properties of egg yolks, especially their sensitivity to heat, should also be considered. Even a little too much heat can scramble egg yolks and mar the smoothness of a dessert. If you add yolks to a hot mixture, do so gradually and stir the mixture vigorously. Any mixture containing yolks should be stirred constantly during cooking.

In addition to the eating appeal of creamy desserts, they are a boon to the busy cook because most can be completely prepared ahead of time.

STRAWBERRY MOUSSE

A fruit mousse is easily made by thickening fruit purée with gelatin and enriching it with whipped cream. This pink mousse is studded with strawberry slices and garnished with whole strawberries. Always remember to hull strawberries only after rinsing them to avoid getting water inside the berries.

1½ pounds strawberries (two 12-oz baskets)
1½ envelopes unflavored gelatin (4½ tsp total)
½ cup water
⅔ cup sugar
1 cup whipping cream

1. Purée half the strawberries in a food processor or blender until very smooth. Pour purée into a large bowl.

2. Sprinkle gelatin over ¼ cup of the water in a small cup and let stand for 5 minutes.

3. In a small saucepan, combine sugar and the remaining ¼ cup water. Stir until thoroughly mixed. Heat over low heat, stirring, until sugar dissolves completely. Raise heat to medium and bring to a boil, stirring. Simmer 30 seconds without stirring.

4. Remove from heat; immediately whisk in softened gelatin, in two portions. Let mixture cool 3 minutes, stirring often.

5. Gradually pour gelatin mixture into strawberry purée, whisking constantly.

6. Refrigerate mixture, stirring often, until it is cold and beginning to thicken but is not set (about 30 minutes).

7. Lightly oil a 6-cup ring mold. Chill mixer bowl and beater for whipping cream. Reserve 8 attractive strawberries for decoration. Slice remaining strawberries crosswise; if any slices are very large, cut them in half. Chill slices and whole berries until ready to use.

8. Stir sliced berries into chilled purée and refrigerate until mixture begins to set, stirring often (about 5 minutes). Remove from refrigerator.

9. Whip cream in chilled bowl with chilled beater until soft peaks form. Gently fold cream into strawberry mixture. Refrigerate 15 minutes, folding mixture occasionally.

10. Pour mixture into ring mold, smoothing top. Cover with plastic wrap. Refrigerate until completely set (about 3 hours).

11. Unmold a short time before serving: Dip mold for about 10 seconds into enough warm water to come nearly to top; pat dry. Run a thin-bladed, flexible knife around edge of dessert, gently pushing dessert slightly from edge of mold to let in air. Set a round serving platter on top of mold, hold tightly, and invert dessert and platter together. Shake mold downward once; mousse should come out onto platter. If dessert remains in mold, repeat procedure. Carefully remove mold by lifting it straight up.

12. Decorate center of dessert with whole strawberries. Refrigerate until ready to serve.

Serves 6 to 8.

Tips

. . . ON WORKING WITH EGGS

Separating Eggs It's easiest to separate eggs when they are cold because the fat in the egg yolk is firmer, making the yolk less likely to break. However, egg whites can be beaten most easily when they are at room temperature. Therefore, when you need to beat egg whites, the best working procedure is to separate the eggs as soon as you remove them from the refrigerator and then leave them at room temperature while preparing the other ingredients for the recipe.

To separate an egg, have ready two small bowls. Crack the egg gently on the counter as close to the center of the egg as possible. If the egg does not crack in half, crack it again once or twice.

Holding half of the shell in each hand, transfer the yolk carefully from one half shell to the other, letting the egg white drip into a bowl. When all of the white has dripped into the bowl, put the yolk in the second bowl. If any yolk gets into the bowl of egg white, use an eggshell half to scoop it out.

Beating Egg Whites The process of beating causes egg whites to trap air bubbles, which will expand in the presence of heat and cause mixtures, such as soufflés, to rise. Uncooked egg whites also add lightness to desserts such as mousses.

For beating egg whites, be sure to use a clean, dry bowl and clean beaters. Beat at low speed at first to stabilize the egg whites. Once they are very foamy, increase the speed to medium-high. Whip until they form stiff peaks but stop before they become lumpy and dry.

If sugar is to be added, do it at high speed and continue beating just until the whites are shiny. They will be very smooth but not dry, which makes it easier to combine them with other ingredients.

Whipped egg whites lose their volume rapidly if allowed to stand. Wait to whip them until you are ready to use them, then fold them immediately into the other ingredients. If you are making a baked dish, baking should follow without delay.

Folding Ingredients When beaten egg whites or whipped cream are to be combined with other ingredients, the recommended procedure is folding. The gentle motion of folding is preferred because it protects the whipped ingredients from deflating. Folding should be done quickly but lightly.

First stir about one fourth of the whites or cream into the heavier mixture to lighten it. The resulting lightened mixture will be easier to blend with the remaining whites or cream because mixtures of similar consistency can be more readily folded together.

Pour the remaining whites or cream on top of the heavier mixture. Fold by moving a large rubber spatula or slotted spoon under the mixture in a clockwise direction and bringing the mixture up over the whites or cream while rotating the bowl counterclockwise at the same time. Repeat this motion several times, just until all the ingredients are blended. It is especially important not to fold egg whites for too long to avoid deflating their air bubbles.

A water bath is used for Baked Chocolate Custard to ensure very gentle cooking and to guard against overheating.

BAKED CHOCOLATE CUSTARD

Custards for baking are set in a water bath, or a pan of hot water in the oven, so that they bake slowly and evenly. These custards are easy to prepare and have a rich chocolate flavor.

> 5 *ounces semisweet chocolate, chopped*
> 2 *cups milk*
> 3 *egg yolks*
> 2 *eggs*
> 6 *tablespoons sugar*

1. Preheat oven to 350° F. Combine chocolate and ½ cup of the milk in the top of a double boiler or in a medium-sized, heatproof bowl. Put hot water in bottom part of double boiler or in a saucepan and set water over low heat. Set container with chocolate mixture above hot water. Leave until chocolate melts, stirring occasionally.

2. Meanwhile, bring the remaining 1½ cups milk to a simmer in a medium saucepan over medium heat.

3. As soon as chocolate melts, remove it from above the hot water and whisk gently until smooth. Gradually pour hot milk into chocolate, stirring; be sure to stir in any chocolate stuck on sides of pan.

4. Whisk egg yolks and eggs lightly in a large bowl. Add sugar and whisk just to blend. Gradually pour in chocolate mixture, whisking constantly. Strain mixture into a large measuring cup. Skim foam from surface of mixture.

5. Set six 5-ounce ramekins in a roasting pan or large, shallow baking dish. Pour custard mixture into ramekins, dividing it evenly among them. Skim any remaining foam from mixture in ramekins.

122

6. Place pan with ramekins in oven. Add enough very hot water to pan to come halfway up sides of ramekins. Set sheet of foil on top to cover ramekins. Bake until custard is nearly set and moves only very slightly when pan is moved gently (about 22 minutes). Or test by inserting a cake tester or the point of a small thin-bladed knife very gently in the mixture about ½ inch from edge of each ramekin. If it comes out clean, the custard is done. During baking, if water in pan comes close to boil, add a few tablespoons cold water to pan and reduce oven temperature to 325° F.

7. Carefully remove ramekins from water bath, place them on a rack, and let cool to room temperature. Refrigerate at least 3 hours before serving. Custards can be kept, covered, up to 1 day in refrigerator. Serve cold, in the ramekins.

Serves 6.

LEMON SOUFFLÉ

Although a baked soufflé must be served immediately, the soufflé base can be made ahead so that the only last-minute work is beating the egg whites and putting the soufflé in the oven. Soufflés are often sprinkled quickly with confectioners' sugar as soon as they come out of the oven. The most efficient way to do this is to put the sugar in a shaker made for this purpose.

1 cup milk
3 egg yolks
6 tablespoons sugar
4 tablespoons flour
2 tablespoons fresh, strained lemon juice
4 teaspoons grated lemon rind
5 egg whites
Confectioners' sugar (optional)

1. Set aside 2 tablespoons of the milk. Bring the remaining milk to a boil in a small, heavy saucepan.

2. In a medium bowl whisk yolks lightly. Add 4 tablespoons of the sugar and the 2 tablespoons reserved milk and whisk until thick and smooth. Stir in flour with whisk.

3. Gradually whisk in half the hot milk. Return mixture to milk in pan, whisking. Cook over low heat, whisking, until mixture comes to a boil.

4. Remove from heat and whisk in lemon juice and rind. If not using immediately, dab mixture with a small piece of butter to prevent a skin from forming. Mixture can be kept, covered, up to 8 hours in refrigerator.

5. Preheat oven to 425° F. Generously butter a 5-cup soufflé dish. Have ready a round, heatproof platter near the oven.

6. Transfer lemon mixture to a heavy saucepan and whisk until smooth. Heat over low heat, whisking, until just hot. Remove from heat.

7. Beat egg whites until stiff. Add the remaining 2 tablespoons sugar, beating at high speed. Continue beating for about 30 seconds.

8. Stir about one quarter of whites into lemon mixture. Spoon this mixture over remaining egg whites and fold together as gently but as quickly as possible, until just blended.

9. Transfer soufflé mixture to buttered soufflé dish and quickly smooth top with spatula. Bake until puffed and browned (about 15 minutes); when you carefully move the dish, the soufflé should shake very gently in the center.

10. Set soufflé dish on platter, sprinkle soufflé with confectioners' sugar, if desired, and serve immediately. Dish up with 2 spoons so that each portion includes some soft center and some firmer crust.

Serves 4.

BASIC CHOCOLATE MOUSSE

Chocolate mousse is a surprisingly easy dessert to prepare. To make it extra festive, pipe a rosette of whipped cream (use half the quantity prepared for Fruit Salad with Liqueur and Whipped Cream, page 117) onto each serving. If you prefer a version without alcohol, substitute water, orange juice, or prepared coffee for the brandy.

7 ounces semisweet or bitter-sweet chocolate, chopped
3 tablespoons brandy
1 tablespoon water
1 tablespoon unsalted butter, at room temperature
4 eggs, separated
1 tablespoon sugar

1. Combine chocolate, brandy, and water in the top of a double boiler or in a medium-sized, heatproof bowl. Put hot water in bottom part of double boiler or in a saucepan and set water over low heat. Set container with chocolate mixture above hot water. Leave until chocolate melts, stirring occasionally. Remove from pan of water and stir until smooth.

2. Add butter to chocolate mixture and stir until well blended.

3. Add one egg yolk and beat it in vigorously with a wooden spoon. Add remaining egg yolks, one by one, in same way.

4. Beat egg whites until fairly stiff. Add sugar, beating at high speed. Continue beating for about 30 seconds.

5. Quickly fold one fourth of whites into chocolate mixture. Gently fold in remaining whites, until just blended.

6. Pour mousse into 4 dessert dishes, small ramekins, or stemmed glasses. Refrigerate until set (about 2 hours). The mousse can be kept, covered, for 2 days in refrigerator.

Serves 4.

INDEX

Note: Page numbers in italics refer to illustrations separated from recipe text.

U.S. MEASURE AND METRIC MEASURE CONVERSION CHART

		Formulas for Exact Measures			Rounded Measures for Quick Reference		
	Symbol	**When you know:**	**Multiply by**	**To find:**			
Mass (Weight)	oz	ounces	28.35	grams	1 oz		= 30 g
	lb	pounds	0.45	kilograms	4 oz		= 115 g
	g	grams	0.035	ounces	8 oz		= 225 g
	kg	kilograms	2.2	pounds	16 oz	= 1 lb	= 450 g
					32 oz	= 2 lb	= 900 g
					36 oz	= 2¼ lb	= 1,000 g (1 kg)
Volume	tsp	teaspoons	5.0	milliliters	¼ tsp	= 1/24 oz	= 1 ml
	tbsp	tablespoons	15.0	milliliters	½ tsp	= 1/12 oz	= 2 ml
	fl oz	fluid ounces	29.57	milliliters	1 tsp	= 1/6 oz	= 5 ml
	c	cups	0.24	liters	1 tbsp	= ½ oz	= 15 ml
	pt	pints	0.47	liters	1 c	= 8 oz	= 250 ml
	qt	quarts	0.95	liters	2 c (1 pt)	= 16 oz	= 500 ml
	gal	gallons	3.785	liters	4 c (1 qt)	= 32 oz	= 1 l.
	ml	milliliters	0.034	fluid ounces	4 qt (1 gal)	= 128 oz	= 3¾ l.
Length	in.	inches	2.54	centimeters	⅜ in.	= 1 cm	
	ft	feet	30.48	centimeters	1 in.	= 2.5 cm	
	yd	yards	0.9144	meters	2 in.	= 5 cm	
	mi	miles	1.609	kilometers	2½ in.	= 6.5 cm	
	km	kilometers	0.621	miles	12 in. (1 ft)	= 30 cm	
	m	meters	1.094	yards	1 yd	= 90 cm	
	cm	centimeters	0.39	inches	100 ft	= 30 m	
					1 mi	= 1.6 km	
Temperature	° F	Fahrenheit	5/9 (after subtracting 32)	Celsius	32° F	= 0° C	
					68 °F	= 20° C	
	° C	Celsius	9/5 (then add 32)	Fahrenheit	212° F	= 100° C	
Area	in.²	square inches	6.452	square centimeters	1 in.²	= 6.5 cm²	
	ft²	square feet	929.0	square centimeters	1 ft²	= 930 cm²	
	yd²	square yards	8,361.0	square centimeters	1 yd²	= 8,360 cm²	
	a	acres	0.4047	hectares	1 a	= 4,050 m²	